SO-CFE-860

Moments
OF
Grace
. . .
Lessons
FROM
Grief

Moments of Grace... Lessons from Grief

ROBERTA CARLSON

Tyndale House
Publishers, Inc.
Wheaton, Illinois

ACKNOWLEDGMENTS

Special thanks are in order to some special people:

To JOHN FORSSMAN *and* KEITH CARLSON *for
suggesting that I look for moments of grace.*

To R.C. *and* VESTA SPROUL, *my brother and
sister-in-law, for the encouragement to write this
story.*

To DONNA BARKER *and* JUDY CARLSON *for
suggesting that I needed to say more about this or less
about that, always with keen insight.*

To HELEN JENSMA *for tackling the computer to get
this manuscript typed.*

And to DAN ELLIOTT, *my editor, for showing me
that editors and probation supervisors
have the same task—
bringing out the best in the raw material
with which they work.*

All Scripture quotations
are taken from
*The Bible in
Today's English Version,*
copyright 1976 by the
American Bible Society.

First printing, August 1987

Library of Congress
Catalog Card Number 87-50500
ISBN 0-8423-4602-3
Copyright 1987 by Roberta Carlson
All rights reserved
Printed in the United States
of America

for BOB *and* SUE

for SHARON, BRENDA, *and* PAM

so that they will be

able to remember

CONTENTS

INTRODUCTION

FOR THOSE who dare to look, pain and grief are never very far away. There is the family whose teenage son finally ends his isolation in a garage filled with carbon monoxide. And the young woman who, just as she senses being able to heal long years of differences with her father, receives the phone call that he has died suddenly of a massive coronary. Or the family whose ten-year-old son falls through thin ice on a pond, never to play again. Or the wife who finds her husband slumped over the wheel of the car, his heart no longer able to sustain life. Or the father who has to watch his thirteen-year-old son die horribly of leukemia before he even has a chance to get used to the idea that the boy is ill. There is the county attorney who walks with her professor husband closely after brushes with death and long hours in the intensive coronary care unit and one day goes home from the hospital alone. And the woman who after her own mastectomy nurses her husband through two years of lung cancer but then is left to run the farm on her own. And the woman widowed many years ago who found another husband to bring joy to her life and is now anticipating a second widowhood as she approaches her own twilight years.

Pain and grief. Sorrow and loss. Feeling helpless, people wonder, "What can I say? What can I do?" It is for these that I write, for people who have experienced this loss so close to themselves, and for those who stand beside the grieving one, wondering how to minister. I write also for myself, as part of my own healing, for I lost a special person not long ago.

I know now that grief is not something to be feared, nor is it an enemy. I have learned that grief is my friend and my teacher. Through grief I have been taught to see in a new way, beyond the actual event that is taking place, to find meaning on a higher level. I call these new insights moments of grace.

A moment of grace is an awareness of God's activity in my life, a moment that causes me to remember his sovereignty, his provision, his faithfulness. It is a moment that helps me make sense out of life, one of those times I say to myself, *Oh, that's what this means!*

Experiencing a moment of grace is like finding an elusive piece of a jigsaw puzzle that, once it is in place, allows a whole section to be completed quickly and easily. Or finally remembering a word that fits the crossword clue, giving me that "Of course!" response.

Moments of grace demand the light of the living

Lord to be recognized. They are not visible to people who can't see or who are in the dark.

If you see yourself or your daughter or your mother or your friend in these words and can, on occasion, nod your head in understanding, I will have accomplished my goal. And perhaps I will have encouraged you to reach out, to make a friend of grief, and to search for your own moments of grace.

O N E
Bobbie

MY HUSBAND is dead. I am not. I must go on, not
holding on to him, gaining identity from him even in
death, but understanding who I am—the gift he gave
me at the cost of his life. He left a legacy that unfolds
daily. His pain was a compass that pointed me to God,
a needle searing itself into my life. This legacy is not for
me only. It is for you as well.

He has been dead for more than a year now, and that
means I have been a widow as long, struggling to carve
out a new understanding for myself, of myself. What
does it mean to be a widow? It isn't exactly every girl's
dream. But it is a reality, a very real fact. This has been
a time of learning, a time of discovery, filled with
moments of grace.

A few weeks ago a good friend was facing surgery. A
suspicious-looking intestinal blockage had been found,
and her doctors felt it was serious enough to operate.
Later her husband called me at work. "Bobbie, Mary Jo
is at Mary Greeley Medical Center. She's OK. She just

had surgery, and a section of her colon was removed. She'd like to see you."

I didn't want to go, not back to MGMC. That's where my husband, John, had spent his last two months, dying. I wasn't sure I could go, be cheerful, encourage my friend, watch her with that awful nasogastric tube in her nose, knowing that every word she spoke rasped her throat. I didn't want to listen to that pump gurgle out stomach fluid. But Mary Jo was my friend. She had reached out to me early on in my grief. Could I do less for her?

I got on the elevator with two nurses. One of them I recognized—her name was Gail. She had cared for John. I hadn't seen her for a year. I looked a little different than I had then, but Gail saw through the cosmetic changes. "Bobbie, how are you?" She turned to her friend. "Do you know who this is? This is John's wife!" A moment of grace—right there in a sterile elevator! A year after his death the nurses still remembered him, still felt the impact of his presence. One of the advantages of a slow death is the chance to touch the lives of others. John did that.

Mary Jo *was* pleased to see me. And I was comfortable being there. We talked. I found I could be glad for her that she didn't have cancer, that she was going to be fine. I found I didn't need her to be unhappy just because I had experienced unhappiness. Another moment of grace! Healing was happening in me as well as in her.

Being a widow is not particularly fun. I found myself making a list of words to describe the phenomenon. They started out mostly negative:

> the pits
> lonely
> overwhelming
> frightening
> stifling

I wondered if I'd ever get moving again. C. S. Lewis was right when he spoke of the laziness of grief.

Now, however, some new words are coming alive:

> opportunity
> understanding
> appreciation
> connection
> compassion

I have been learning that participation in another's suffering gives meaning both to the other and to me and cements us together in a way few other things can. My eyes have been opened to the myriad disguises that pain wears in our world. I realize I cannot touch it all, but I can touch some of it. There *is* life.

Before this experience I did not know why the Bible spoke of a Suffering Servant, of taking up a cross, of learning obedience, of not being afraid. I continue to be amazed at how many times in the Word when something happens it is introduced by, "Don't be afraid." Fear is the antithesis of life. Fear paralyzes and kills. The awareness of moments of grace, however, encourages me and spurs me on.

Moments of grace lead to victory. Victory is the motif I hear the holy God sounding out over and over in his Word. A hundred different ways he tells me, "I will not forsake you," "I will be with you," "I will not leave you comfortless." God is talking to me: "Bobbie, Bobbie, trust me. I will not forsake you." I have learned to believe him.

I used to think that God wasn't there, or that if he was he didn't really care about me. I looked to others for strength and leadership and relationships to give me meaning. I didn't sense any real meaning of my own. I was always someone's daughter, someone's wife, someone's sister, someone's mother. Take away those modifiers and who was I? And especially when I found John I found incarnate strength, vision, tenderness, joy. He was my pearl of great price. And—wonder of wonders—*I* was precious to *him*. How could that be? I couldn't believe it. I didn't trust him for a long time. It was indeed too good to be true.

Part of this story is my story and part of it is John's story—his quest for "Quality." That is what he called what he was looking for. He never stopped that search to find meaning for his life.

I first met John Carlson on October 4, 1975. He was a volunteer probation supervisor for the Committee on Criminal Justice (CCJ), and I was the new assistant coordinator. I came to CCJ not knowing exactly what to expect. In 1975 I was thirty-nine years old. I was one year out of college, and this was my first real job.

I had been voted the girl most likely to succeed in my high school graduating class of 1954. Like many of my classmates, I went on to college. My first year I studied at Westminster College in New Wilmington, Pennsylvania. It was a small school of about one thousand students. My freshman class of 317 had only two more students than my senior class at Clairton (Pa.) High School. School was easy for me academically but difficult socially. My high-school boyfriend had chosen to attend Carnegie Tech in Pittsburgh. That was seventy miles from New Wilmington.

Late in the fall of 1954 an event happened that changed my life drastically. My father had the first in a series of strokes and heart attacks that eventually took his life two years later. He was fifty-one at the time. In order to be closer to my suburban Pittsburgh home, I transferred to Carnegie Tech. School was still relatively easy, and now my social life was better as well because I was closer to my boyfriend.

Our relationship did not progress smoothly, however. I was struggling even then with accepting myself. I did not believe that anyone could love me for myself, that I was acceptable. I did what so many others have done: I bought belonging at the price of my body. At nineteen I was pregnant and unmarried. Of course we did the proper thing. We were married quietly in a simple private service.

I had gone to church all my life until this time. I knew much about God, but I didn't know him. That wouldn't come until nearly twenty-five years later. I didn't know how to talk to God, but I remember bargaining with him about this situation. I knew I would be the one who would have to drop out of school while my new husband would go on to graduate and then pursue his PhD. I didn't think this was quite fair, and I told God so. But he seemed not to be listening to me because he didn't do anything to change things. At that time I began to have some serious doubts about all this business I had learned at church. But I never told anyone.

Early in November 1956, on a Friday, my father suffered another stroke and lay at home in a coma. I sat with him for a while on Sunday, horrified at the sound of such labored breathing, yet not knowing what to do or who to talk to. I did not want to be in that room with my father. He was no longer the vibrant man I had known.

He died at nine on Monday evening, November 5. I was not told until the following morning. I was angry about that. During the funeral preparations I was encouraged not to be at the funeral home to greet people. No one ever said anything about my condition, but I was sure that I was being kept away because my advanced pregnancy would be an embarrassment for the family and the mourners. At the time of the funeral, the family sat in a separate room away from the others. Again I felt I was being hidden.

My father had been special to me, and I knew I had been special to him. Inside myself I was sure that his death was my punishment from God for being so evil as to get pregnant without being married. Again, I never said this to anyone, and I became convinced that I would not survive the birth of my child.

Ten days later, on November 16, 1956, I was admitted to the hospital to have my baby. Since both my husband and I were underage in Pennsylvania, my mother had to come to the hospital to sign for any medication I would be given. The new widow willingly made the trip and then waited for her first grandchild. Shortly after my son was born, a nurse came to my mother. "Do you have a reverend?" she asked. My mother nodded. "Then you'd better call him," the nurse went on. "Your daughter is dying."

Well, my severe bleeding was brought under control and I didn't die. There were many times during those first few years of marriage, however, when I wished I had died. I knew how guilty I felt. I knew I had killed my father. And I knew my life was out of my control. I also knew my husband had married me only because he had to. I didn't understand at the time that most of this wasn't true.

In an attempt to atone for the immense guilt I was feeling, I gave up responsibility for myself. I thought if

I allowed others—my husband, his parents, our friends—to guide my decisions, things would be all right and I would be able to get rid of some of the guilt I felt. If I made no decisions, I could incur no new guilt.

I was deeply ashamed of my behavior and I knew God couldn't forgive me. I knew I was unlovable, so I allowed no one to love me. I allowed no one to get close enough to see the desperation inside. In all of this, I knew I was displeasing God, but I had no idea what to do about it.

Thus began a decade of trying to please people. I would shape my behavior around others and what they thought was important. Things went well for quite a long time. I became proficient at my game.

During these years I began doing volunteer work, most of it in the church. I began working with junior-high youth—teaching church school, developing midweek programs, writing and directing plays, leading retreats. These young people became very important to me. Through them I gained some of the appreciation that I was lacking in other areas of my life. I took my young son along on outings with the youth. The church became a symbol of the place that I could get recognition. I was hungry for that and spent many hours developing ways to keep myself busy there.

All of that vanished in 1962 when we moved from Pennsylvania to Iowa. As could be expected, my

professor husband had a ready-made group of colleagues to join at Iowa State University, but I started
out with no one. I don't do well in a new environment.
I went to the only place I knew to get connected to
people: the church.

After a few months I was just beginning to meet
some new people when we moved again, this time to
northern Virginia. Again it was my husband's needs
that precipitated the move. He had to serve his time on
active duty for the army. Once again, in order to find a
place where I could be myself, I looked to the church.
And once again, my talents in working with youth
were noticed and put to work.

Twice during this two-year stay I became pregnant
again and twice miscarried. When the time came
to return to Iowa, my doctor insisted I make the trip
by air. Upon arrival this time the first place I went
was to the doctor. It took several months to regain my
strength after that second miscarriage and its com-
plications. But at least we had a church to which to
return.

Once again I found myself with the junior highers.
The next three years were my most active and fulfilling
years up to that time. The youth program we developed
was a wonderful success. Many young people came out
every Wednesday after school and stayed until seven-
thirty or eight, fully involved in an active and diver-
sified program. The adults functioned as a team in
preparing for this program and developed rapport with

the youth. It was a wonderful experience.

During this time, though, I began to notice that I was only "myself" when I was with these kids. No longer did I feel this way at home. My husband was not always supportive of the time I gave to the youth program and the people connected with it. But I looked forward to it more than anything else.

In 1967 two things happened. One was a releasing, the other was a taking away. My daughter Sue was born in May. She weighed seven pounds seven ounces. I saw that as a sign from God that I had been forgiven for my sin nearly eleven years earlier. I saw her birth weight as the seventy times seven of which Jesus had spoken.

The day before she was born, I spent my last time as a junior high teacher. The church had a three-year rule. A person holding a position for three years then had to sit out a year before doing that particular task again. I was due a year out.

I did have other jobs in the congregation: I sang in the choir, was president of the women's group, sat on the Christian Education Committee. I also served on the board of the local YWCA and became involved in other community groups. But I no longer had "my kids," those junior highers who had given me a reason to be. I felt that every time I found something wonderful it was taken away from me. I felt increasingly worthless.

My husband's department at the university had a

group for the wives of both faculty members and graduate students. (At that time there were no women on the staff, nor were there any female graduate students.) When each new year would start and all the women would introduce themselves, the second question would always be, "And what is your degree in?" I got tired of answering, "I didn't graduate from college." I began to think of returning to school to finish my degree. That, however, was expensive. We were always, it seemed, struggling to make our income last all month. And two children take a lot of time and care. I could think of a hundred reasons why I couldn't go back to school. Besides, if I finished my degree, I would lose a good gripe. It was not yet time.

As a young teenager, I had been encouraged by my father to go to a high school in a neighboring mill town. Students in our class had a choice. We could attend either a nice, suburban, middle-class high school in Brentwood or the larger, more diverse one in Clairton. My father, with wisdom, had recommended Clairton for me. It was my first exposure to people from a wide range of socioeconomic backgrounds.

The second dynamic exposure came in 1967 in Ames, Iowa. A social worker came up with the idea that it would be good to blend together women from lower and middle income groups. The plan was to have them meet together with their preschool children one morning a week. The children would have a day-care experience together and the mothers would do such things as learn how to make new and intriguing meals from the same old peanut butter and canned meat that were government surplus foods in that day. The plans also included talking about child care, family finances, birthday parties, housecleaning, making instead of buying gifts, and anything else that seemed important to the various women. The group met every Wednesday morning and was known as Wednesday Morning Club.

It was in this group that I was introduced to the horror of child abuse. The first time I saw a child with small, circular burns on her arms and chest, I didn't know that they were from cigarettes. I didn't know that some people deliberately harm children. I had never been exposed to that kind of behavior.

It was also in this group that I began to see how people learn to cope with heavy burdens. I met first, second, and even third generation welfare mothers. I saw a hopelessness in their eyes. I saw how some of them had learned to be helpless and how they used others to get what they wanted. I saw and interacted with women who took no active part in their own lives. They were as spectators watching events pass before them. As long as they could stay alive without taking responsibility for themselves, they would. They were experts at placing blame outside themselves: things happened to them. They had no part in the process at all, except to be acted upon. I saw part of myself in them and would recall that attitude later when I was struggling with my own grief.

In Wednesday Morning Club I met Helen, a woman
unable to read. I had learned previously that Iowa has
the highest literacy rate in the nation, 99 percent. But
Helen was one of the one percent. She had gone to
school for only six years, and hers was a limited world.
I began to take another look at education and the
barriers that it could remove. I also continued to
complain about never having finished my degree.

One night I was seated at the table in the home of
some friends repeating my now-familiar litany when
my husband said, "Why don't you quit complaining
about it and go back to school?" The next day I went to
the admissions office at Iowa State University and
applied for admission as a part-time student. It was
November 1970. I was accepted as a junior to begin
classes in winter quarter 1971. All my courses from
Westminster and Carnegie Tech had transferred even
though fifteen years had elapsed. I enrolled with a
double major in philosophy and speech.

It took me eleven quarters to do two years' work.
Halfway through I changed my emphasis, made
philosophy a minor, and began taking all of the cross-
disciplinary courses that the university offered in the
area of linguistics. I also took a part-time job to help
defray the cost of tuition. I used to tell my friends that I
was going to school half time, working half time and
taking care of my family half time.

I did well in school. I worked hard and got the extra
help I needed with courses that required a lot of

mathematics. But I did it, and did it well. Some of the confidence I had lost a decade and a half earlier was beginning to return. I was fascinated by new ideas, new ways of looking at my world, and was basking in the warmth of my professors' favor. I was learning that I could think for myself. More important, I was learning that I *could* think. I had accepted for too long that mine was only the emotional response to life. Now I discovered that I was able to be logical, to reason for myself. The change in myself and my awareness of the world was becoming apparent.

During this time in my life I had nothing to do with the church and, especially, nothing to do with God. Shortly before I had started back to school, I had undergone a bad experience at church. After my one-year sabbatical from teaching, I was once again asked to be part of a team of youth leaders, this time with an experimental group of eleventh and twelfth graders from the two Presbyterian churches in Ames. The youth from my church had grown up in the church and had been part of my former Wednesday night program. The youth from the other church were not regular church attenders. Some were unchurched except for this exposure. Though the two groups went to the same high school, they were not part of the same crowd.

The leadership for the group was six adults—the associate pastor, two young married couples, and me.

We struggled together to work out a curriculum for the teens.

The community was overshadowed by the social unrest of 1969. On a national level, the memory of the assassinations of Bobby Kennedy and Martin Luther King, Jr., were still clear. Ames was being torn apart by local issues as well. Calls for help came to churches because of a boycott of campus buildings and programs by black students. Opposition to the Vietnam War was growing, and the Ames City Hall had been bombed. Our plans for the church youth program sparked disagreement. Half the group of senior highers wanted to deal with social issues. The other half was content to do "normal" youth group activities.

The inevitable clash came at a retreat when one of the young couples and some of the youth declared they wouldn't be a part of the group if I had anything to do with it. This statement began a period of several months that was painful for all in the group. After much discussion among the youth, and between the youth and adult leaders, the decision was reached to try to work together. By being willing to do the difficult thing, we learned that we could find both openness and closeness—another lesson I would remember later.

Not all the members of my church were so openhearted. There were many harsh words, mis-understandings on all sides, and, on my part, neither

wisdom nor kindness. I thought I knew all about
working with kids. I had been doing so for most of the
preceding twelve years. But in that time I had not
understood much of what I had been teaching those
kids. I had quite a bit of knowledge *about* the Scriptures
and events in Jesus' life. But I hadn't personally encoun-
tered the living Lord, the sovereign God.

What happened next was a deep, deep split in our
pastorless congregation, and groups of people from
both sides of the controversy left the church. I saw this
as the worst thing that had ever happened to me. The
Christian Education Committee ruled that I would
never again be allowed to work with senior high youth.
I became very bitter and within two years asked for my
membership to be canceled. If God didn't want me, I
didn't want him either.

I lived that way, without God, for more than a
decade. I lived with flexible standards, with values that
changed to fit the situation. At first it was tremendously
freeing. I did not have to be and act like some stodgy
old institution said. I could decide for myself what was
true, what was right. I looked to my professors in the
classes I was taking at Iowa State. I read, listened, tried
new ways of behaving, of thinking. I lived in a relativis-
tic world.

In 1974, twenty years after graduating from high
school, I graduated from college. I was the top graduating senior in the Department of Speech that year. I had
experienced positive feedback from my teachers and

had come face-to-face with exciting ways of thinking about the problems I saw around me. I no longer looked out on a pristine world. These were the days of Watergate and further deterioration of the nation's moral climate. For me, the church and God were dead, and my country had lost its virginity. Was there really such a thing as Truth with a capital *T?* I thought that anyone who believed so was stupid at best, and I scoffed at such naiveté when I met it.

I had not, however, reckoned with a sovereign God and a living Lord. On September 15, 1975, my first day working at Committee for Criminal Justice (CCJ), the stage was set for the unfolding of God's plan for me.

CCJ was still a new idea then—a private, nonprofit community corrections agency that saw the necessity of providing a way for people in the community to become involved with the criminal justice system. The commitment of the agency was to treat those in conflict with the law with dignity, and to work at restoring them to the community with long-term, supportive, one-on-one relationships with trained volunteers. I had been hired to train volunteers and oversee their relationships with clients. I would also have clients of my own, adults who had been granted probation after having committed a crime.

My first day on the job I was assigned a man who had been arrested for drunk driving. He was to be under my supervision, and the court had ordered inpatient treatment for alcoholism. The day we met,

Steve was to report to the hospital. This was my first experience with someone who had been labeled alcoholic. Forty-two days later, when Steve graduated from the program at the hospital, I saw for myself the change that occurs in skin tone, health, and outlook in a recovering alcoholic. Steve was the first of many I saw through that process.

The Magistrate's Court in Ames slowly saw CCJ as an alternative to the regular system. The judges began to send us people to supervise directly. We began working out restitution plans that our clients could follow to repay their victims, and as the program grew we developed programs of financial counseling for individuals and families. Next we moved to setting up community service placements where our probationers could perform volunteer service to repay the community for their misdeeds. In another new program, an alternative to court proceedings, two persons or groups could work out their own solutions to their problems in the presence of a trained mediator.

Two weeks after I started work, my supervisor went on vacation and left me in charge. On October 4, several of our volunteers gathered for a trip to the Iowa Men's Reformatory at Anamosa. That was the day I met John Carlson.

TWO

John

JOHN WAS BORN on August 9, 1944, the fourth child of Dorothy and Reuben Carlson. Reuben was a first generation American. His father, John A. Carlson, for whom Reuben's youngest child was named, had come from Sweden and settled in the rolling hills of eastern Boone County, Iowa. It has been said that the area reminded Grandpa Carlson of home in Sweden. The incredible black soil he found would grow anything, in abundance.

John was the child of Reuben and Dorothy's later years. In 1944 Reuben was fifty-one and Dorothy was forty-three. Their oldest child, Dean, was fifteen, Rosemary was thirteen, and Priscilla was seven.

John had a fairly normal Iowa farm life for his first years of childhood. Things changed in 1952, however, when Reuben died. Dorothy was left to raise the seven-year-old boy. Though fatherless, John had many of the same experiences as other young boys. He had plenty of cob fights with his cousin Keith, who lived a half mile south on the original homestead. And he teased Priscilla mercilessly when she entertained her "young man." He was the typical seven-years-younger kid brother.

John's favorite spot on the farm was the highest spot—the top of the knoll out in the pasture. He spent hours there as he grew up, reading Zane Grey westerns, driving his homemade carts down the hill into a herd of cows, or simply thinking. John did a lot of thinking and wondering about things.

In many ways Keith and Dean became the male role models in John's life, somewhat filling the void left by his father's early death. Dean was especially good with wiring and electricity. He taught John much that he would use later in his mobile home business. Dean was also expert at fixing things. He was the one who had taken over the farm and maintained all the buildings and machinery.

Keith was someone John could talk to. He was nine years older than John, and John observed him closely to see what a teenager was like. He watched Keith go off to college and into the army. He watched Keith marry Judy. He watched Keith begin to wonder about the way things were and how he could help in the world. Keith heard about CCJ first and told John about it. Their lives were intertwined in many ways.

When Grandma and Grandpa Carlson were new to Boone County and beginning their farming and family,

they drove the buggy twelve miles into the town of
Boone to the Swedish church services. They were
charter members in 1884 of the newly formed body
now known as the Evangelical Free Church. But they
felt that their American-born children should go to an
American church.

Two and a half miles north of the homestead was the
crossroads that was the little town of Mackey. In 1885,
just north of that intersection, the Mackey Methodist
Church was begun. Grandma and Grandpa Carlson
saw to it that their children were brought up in that
church. So when Reuben brought his bride, Dorothy,
to the Mackey area, she attended that church as well.
John was a member there all his life. He went to Sunday
school as a child, attended youth programs as a teenager, wore bathrobes in numerous Christmas pageants,
built the bathroom addition to the building, and
helped Keith and Judy handle the income from the
annual Mackey Methodist Bazaar.

Mackey was a small, typical rural church—the
center of activity for people in the area. Sometimes the
minister was paid in eggs, sweet corn, and tomatoes. A
few key families—the Carlsons, the Conards, the
Mackeys, the Smalleys—were the mainstay of the
church. The values of good, stable Iowa farm life were
taught there, woven in with the Bible stories of heros
and heroines. This was the background John brought
with him into adulthood when he first began to go
beyond the confines of rural Boone County.

John wanted to go to college. He saw in Keith the benefits that higher education could bring and he aspired to these. The best word to describe John would be *curious*. John's curiosity was insatiable. If he found something to be learned, he would learn it—though not always in the typical fashion. Once he set his mind on going to school, he was not to be stopped. Lack of money was a problem, but John was no stranger to work. He took a job with a mobile home sales and service business. He learned how to transport new mobile homes, set them up, skirt them, and, eventually, to attach and fix everything inside.

John began his college career at what was then Boone Community College. He could commute to classes, continue working, and even save some money. After earning an Associate of Arts degree, he transferred to Iowa State University in nearby Ames. He commuted the fourteen miles to school, continued working part time, and graduated in 1968 with a degree in sociology.

John joined the army's ROTC at Iowa State. He had a deep commitment to his country. He would be ready to serve if it became necessary.

One of his jobs while attending school took him to southern Iowa, where he was helping to set up modular schoolrooms in a small town. While there he met a young woman who was just finishing high school. John had, up to this time, been too busy to notice many girls. He had had a few dates, but there had not been anyone special. He was looking ahead to going on active duty with the army. But this southern Iowa girl was special, he thought. She was patient, kind, and eager to please him. Perhaps she would be the one to become his wife.

A long-distance romance developed and continued to grow. John would work in southern Iowa on the weekends, see his girlfriend, and return home to attend classes during the week. Early in the summer he was ordered to Georgia to attend basic training and Ranger school. Letters kept the young couple in touch. Finally in September 1968, when he was twenty-four and she was eighteen, they were married. He was handsome in his dress blues, a young lieutenant soon to be seeing active duty in the jungles of Vietnam.

John was a good soldier and a good officer. He understood the concepts of leadership, and he knew what it meant to take responsibility. He could, like the soldier in Luke 7, both give and take orders. He did that in Vietnam.

To many Americans who had known war only as it was fought in World War II, the television program "M.A.S.H." made clear the role of the helicopter in modern warfare. John learned about those helicopters firsthand in Southeast Asia. One day he watched a wounded American soldier being airlifted from the combat zone when a sniper's bullet severed the cable pulling his stretcher up into the chopper. He fell into the jungle about five hundred yards from John. John wasted no time. He asked for a volunteer and the two of them headed in the direction that the wounded soldier had fallen. They reached him and rescued him.

Before finishing his time in the army, John would rise to the rank of captain. But at the time of this rescue he was a first lieutenant and platoon leader. His was the responsibility of choosing the man to send on patrol and, perhaps, to his death. John faced and saw death daily. He wondered each day if it would be his last.

One day, four months into his tour, his men lost their leader. Shrapnel from an exploding shell tore into John's torso, arm, throat, face, and eye. Now he was the one to be placed on a stretcher and evacuated from the war. Removed from that hell, he came home scarred, needing healing both physically and emotionally.

They say that war changes a man. This was true for John. In Vietnam he met a side of himself he didn't want to acknowledge. He found inside himself an evil that was willing to kill, even wanting to kill. He never talked much about the time he spent there. I remember only two or three occasions when, years later after we were married, he spoke of the horror of it. Once in a particularly quiet moment he told me how he grew to hate the futility of the whole situation. He hated how his view of himself had been twisted. He hated remembering how much he wanted to kill those people. He was afraid he had lost the ability to be a caring, compassionate human being. As he held me close, he told me about rescuing the soldier who fell. He held me tightly and cried.

Vietnam was a shattering experience for that young twenty-five-year-old man, one that he spent much of the rest of his life atoning for. John was awarded the Purple Heart and the Bronze Star for his work in Vietnam. But he didn't find Quality there. His search for that became most important.

When John spoke of Quality, it was obvious from his voice that this Quality began with a capital Q. But it always seemed to elude him. He had trouble putting into words the concept that was in his head. It was as if even he didn't know exactly what it was, but he would know it when he found it. I know that eventually he did find it, his elusive Quality. He found it in his dying.

After leaving Vietnam, John spent time in a hospital in Tokyo and then in an army hospital in Colorado. The piece of shrapnel that had entered his eye was lodged against the retina. It was copper, not steel, so it could not be removed with a magnet. The ophthalmologist working on the case did not want to risk the loss of his eye. That meant that the rest of John's tour of duty would be in the United States, out of the combat zone.

John and his wife moved to Annandale, Virginia, in 1970. In November his first daughter, Sharon, was born at DeWitt Army Hospital at Fort Belvoir. Captain Carlson liked northern Virginia. He considered staying when it was time to be separated from the service, and he had an opportunity to get into the mobile home business there.

Before making the final decision, the family returned to visit Iowa. John realized then that he wouldn't be staying in the East. His roots went deep into Iowa soil. He had to come home.

During the next five years John ran his own business, Carlson Mobile Home Service. Two more girls, Brenda and Pam, were added to his family. He also became involved with the Committee on Criminal Justice, and that is how we met.

My first impression of him that day we went to the Men's Reformatory was one of an intense person searching. He didn't say much at first but simply loaded as many people as possible into his green van marked CARLSON MOBILE HOME SERVICE. He had a cousin with him—my first indication of strong family ties among the Carlsons.

When we arrived at the reformatory we were met by the warden and introduced to our guide and those armed officers who would serve as our front and rear guards. We were told what to expect and how to be-have. I noticed that John asked questions incessantly. Usually they were searching and bold, the kind of questions that most of the rest of us had in our minds but would not dream of vocalizing. As he probed and learned, he also opened himself. I was intrigued.

Part of CCJ's service to Story County was securing and monitoring employment for people who, prior to any court proceedings, were in the county jail and unable to meet bond. (In 1975 pretrial services in Ames were not operating as they are today. Now the court may decide to release a person pretrial on several levels of supervision with no money paid for the bond.) An accused person would be released at 7:30 A.M. for work and would be expected to be back in jail by 4:45 P.M.

It was difficult to find an employer to match those hours. But my supervisor, Lynette, and I knew that we could call on John to hire a client at almost any time. John, as owner of his own business, was free to be flexible to meet those conditions. CCJ became an opportunity for John to act out the theories he had learned while studying sociology, a way he could do something to help.

John's search went on during those years. I remember words like *happiness, value, feelings,* and, of course, *Quality*—and question after question about what life was all about. Vietnam had changed him. It had changed the way he saw life, the way he saw himself, and the way he saw other people. It had changed his priorities. He would not allow himself to be satisfied with the "good enough." He pushed on for that Quality he needed.

I, also, was searching during those years. My work at CCJ was teaching me much about people and problems and coping skills. CCJ was gaining a reputation for dependability and quality with the judges, attorneys,

and law enforcement people in the county. I was
learning that I could have a positive impact on people.
I was also learning more about hopelessness, helplessness, frenzy to make sense out of life, futility, depres-
sion, and darkness. I was watching people destroy
themselves with alcohol, drugs, and violence because
they didn't know any other way to live. I learned how
expensive change is, how long a process and struggle.
But I also saw it happen.

In reflecting on these experiences, I began to see
how much I had allowed myself to be stifled, to be
shaped and formed and molded by those who touched
my life. Obviously, many of my relationships had been
good ones. But some were not.

One day in the spring of 1977, John asked me the
question that broke my life open. "Bobbie," he said,
"has anyone ever really loved you?" With those words
he stripped away my facade. We had been having a
heated discussion about what course of action to take
with a particularly difficult client. He and I were not in
agreement. We were each holding to our own ideas,
born of our own value systems. I was arguing that this
client should be restrained, not allowed to continue
harming the people around her. She was deeply involved in drugs, alcohol, and incest, and had a history
of serious mental illness. John was arguing that she
needed a model of how to live, not another punishment. She needed to understand that she was loved.
That was the context in which he spoke those words

that ripped into me, into my deepest, dearest place where only I had the right to enter. For me it was an experience on the human level like that of Isaiah when he saw the majestic presence of God. "Woe is me, for I am undone," he said. I was undone as well.

If I can point to a time that was the turning point of my life, it was that moment. I had no idea that this question would eventually lead me to an encounter with God. I didn't know what was in store for me over the next few years. I didn't know then that the fault was mine for not allowing anyone to love me. I didn't know then that a year later, in 1978, I would walk out of my marriage of twenty-two years, and two years after that become the wife of this man who had just cut through to my innermost being. But that is what happened.

God and I were still enemies. Ever since I had abandoned him years earlier I had felt no necessity to do things his way. His Word was not my standard. The world says it is permissible to divorce a spouse when "the thrill is gone," or if you "need to find yourself." I didn't think I had any identity in my marriage. My perception was one of moving in a different direction from my husband. I felt no sense of togetherness. I wanted to try out the new ideas I had learned in school and on the job, to find this new me. Even with that, I thought about leaving for months before I actually did it. My son Bob was away at college and my daughter Sue was just short of her twelfth birthday when I moved out of that home.

With hawklike hindsight I can see quite clearly that my divorce did not please God. Were I to marry again, it would not be an option. But I have been forgiven for that insult to God, my arrogance in thinking that I knew better than he what was right. I have learned that, through God's forgiveness, the past has no power over me anymore.

During the four years between 1976 and 1980, John was searching as well. He was spending less and less time at home. He became deeply involved in his volunteer work at CCJ. He continued to supervise probationers and joined the board of directors. He sold his business and ran the repair and service department for a local mobile home dealer. He was always coming up with new ideas for us to try at CCJ, and he would often drop in at the office to talk about them with Lynette and me. He even took charge of the move when we relocated our offices.

In the early summer of 1977, John applied for a position as a probation officer in the Ames office of the Department of Correctional Services (Iowa's official adult probation agency). In August, John became the Adult Probation Officer for Boone County. As he spent his first few months on the job, he began to see that what CCJ had done in Story County could also be done next door in Boone County.

John was not the kind of probation officer who sat in his office and had all his clients come to him. He was more like an old-time circuit preacher. He went all over the county meeting people in their homes, on the job, or anywhere the two could get together. John had a special booth in a restaurant where clients knew they could find him on certain days and stop for a cup of coffee. The things they expressed showed him that the human service organizations of that community needed to widen their vision.

John discussed his ideas with Lynette and me at CCJ, and together we laid the foundation for a similar program (then called Community Contact Services) to be set up in Boone. John mobilized key community leaders in Boone to form the first board of directors for CCS. (In 1983, just a few months before his death, John was named the Outstanding Correctional Officer of the Year by the Iowa Corrections Association.)

John was struggling these years, trying to understand "the meaning of it all." He thought if people only *knew*, they could and would change those things in their lives that kept them from Quality. He was tireless in his quest—finding Quality became his number one priority. His wife did not seem to share his vision. We often saw him with one or more of his daughters but less and less with his wife, and he began to talk with Lynette and me of divorce.

A few months later, John left his wife, moved out of his home in the country, and filed for divorce.

The question of child custody was not settled for several months. John desperately wanted to gain

custody of the girls. Even though the laws of Iowa
allow fathers that right, mothers are usually granted
custody of children, especially if they are girls. Custody
in this case was granted to the mother, and the divorce
was finalized. But John vowed to himself that he would
never leave the girls. He would do whatever it took to
keep as actively involved in their lives as possible.

John and I began to spend more time getting to
know each other. We talked much of such things as
trust and love. We talked of how I always looked at
events as win-lose situations, while he would hunt for
the win-win possibility. Many times he told me how
precious I was to him. We spoke about what we thought
marriage was supposed to be like—a partnership, a
team, two who trusted each other and would be there
for each other. We thought we had those qualities in
our relationship. I knew I wanted to be this man's wife.
And I was astonished to learn that he wanted me. Early
in 1980 John and I decided we would marry.

I was finally beginning to believe John when he said,
"I love you." He told me once that I had that sentence
twisted all around. He said I kept placing the emphasis
on the *I* or the *love* when it actually belonged on the
you. When he told me he loved me, he was saying he
loved *me*. There it was again, someone trying to break
through and get me to allow them to love me. It was an
incredible concept for me. How could anyone love *me*
after all I had done? I shook my head many times and

went on, not understanding it but even more appreciating its effect on my life.

We needed to find a pastor to officiate at our wedding. There was no regular pastor at the Mackey Church in 1980. John hadn't been going to church much during this time anyway. I still had no church (and no God, either). But John and I had developed a friendship with Dave Crow, pastor of the Presbyterian Church in Boone, when we worked together to set up Community Contact Services. We went to Dave and asked him if he would officiate. After much discussion and several counseling sessions, Dave agreed to do it. Neither of us could take time off work then, and Dave's schedule was full except for the early evening of February 14, 1980.

So, on Valentine's Day, I became Mrs. John Carlson in a private ceremony performed in the chapel of the Presbyterian Church in Boone, before God—a God I still didn't know. John's brother Dean stood up with him. Pat Hayes, a friend from both CCJ and CCS, stood up with me. Dean's wife, Helen, and their daughter Terry were there. My daughter, Sue, was with me. For John and me, it was the beginning of our dream together.

THREE

The Beginning of the Dream

AFTER JOHN AND I were married, it became obvious that we could never live in my home in town. We had no room for a garden or a shop. Besides, town was no place for John, so we began the search for "our" place. Yet no matter what we looked at, it lacked something that John felt was necessary. It didn't take me too long to figure out that we would not be buying our place somewhere else, because John's heart was still on that farm a half mile north of Grandpa Carlson's homestead. In May 1980 John's first wife found employment in a neighboring town and decided to move closer to her work. She and the girls left the farm, freeing it for John and me. For the second time John bought that double-wide mobile home sitting on the farm. (Later I realized this act was a human reminder of God's redemption of his people. They are his because he made them and

doubly his because he redeemed them. John had redeemed his home, and now it was to be my home as well.)

It was not easy moving into what had been John's
home with his first family. His mom's house was less
than twenty yards away. She had not been pleased with
him when he began talking about divorce, was not
pleased with him for going through with it, and was
especially displeased when he suggested bringing his
new wife to that place. John and his mother shared one
trait that was unmistakable. Each was the personification of stubbornness.

A quarter mile to the east lived Dean and Helen,
separated from us by a field that alternately grew corn,
beans, and alfalfa. A half mile south on the original
homestead lived Keith and Judy. Also on that property,
in another double-wide mobile home that John had set
up, lived Florence and Lester Carlson, Keith's aging
parents. It was Florence who welcomed me into the
Carlson clan. She was a special lady who could see
beyond the moment. She would give me much perspective in the years ahead.

John and I gutted the mobile home. We replaced
all the kitchen appliances, put up wallboard in the
living room and three bedrooms, recarpeted everything
but the living room—in short, made it as much *our*
place as we could.

We began to talk about and plan our dream, a passive
solar home, partially earth-sheltered—a magnificent
hole in the ground that we would live in. We would

take the mobile home apart and put it over the hole and then redo it so that Sharon, Brenda, Pam, and Sue would have their own bedrooms when they were with us every other weekend. Our home would be heated year-round by the sun and our wood/coal-burning stove. It would be wonderful. It would have a shop for John to tinker in and get serious about making furniture. And, best of all for me, it would have a tornado room, a place where I could escape the terror of those violent storms.

The girls thought it was great, too, and joined in as we walked out and surveyed the boundaries of the hole. However, to begin construction of our dream, we had to own the land. After much discussion and pleading, John's mom agreed to sell us one acre of the farm. Dean, Rosemary, and Priscilla agreed as well. That acre—roughly 85 feet by 512 feet—became ours. In the spring of 1981 we dug the hole.

John was determined that we do as much of the work on our house as we were able. Our work began with building and painting the forms for the concrete walls. John found a store that was selling out all its remnant cans of paint. He bought them and we used them to paint the forms. The men who brought the concrete were amused to be greeted with lavender, mint, pink, cream, aqua, and chartreuse vessels awaiting their product. But colors didn't stop the forms from performing their task. Our walls were straight, secure, and strong.

As we were laying the foundation for our home, we were also laying the foundations for blending our two families together and giving form to our mutual quest, which we began to see as a spiritual one. John had done a good job both in telling me and showing me that it was necessary to have standards. All the measuring and planning needed to make sure a building would stand served as a good object lesson. He scoffed when I argued that there was no such thing as Truth. "Bobbie, that's ridiculous," he would say. "You've got to have a standard to measure by. You can't even know truths without a definition of Truth." I was smart enough to see where my reasoning would take me, and I realized that the God I had been insisting was not there for a decade was going to have to be reckoned with.

Dave Crow decided to begin a spiritual growth group in his congregation in Boone. When John learned of it, he asked Dave if it would be all right to have some outsiders there. Dave said that it would be fine. John and I went without having any idea what a spiritual growth group was. Of the seven people there, five of us were outsiders. As we met together we looked at New Testament parables that began, "The Kingdom of heaven is like. . . ." After Bible study we spent time in directed, meditative prayer, learning to visualize ideas and concepts. I found it thrilling, and John asked questions tirelessly.

As our new house grew, so did this new house of

spiritual understanding. We began to go to church at Mackey, where John had friends, since it was the Carlsons' home church. We met Jerry and Sharon Mumm and their two children there. They would become close and dear to us over the next two years. I did not join the church nor did I participate in the sacrament of the Lord's Supper. I wasn't yet ready for that.

By October 1981 our hole in the ground was ready to have the mobile home split into its two parts and rejoined in its position atop the new walls. John directed that job with his usual flair but was foiled in his attempt by an early snow squall that left the second half of our house out in the adjacent cornfield, now too slick for the truck to get enough traction to back it into position. For two days we lived in half a house with the openings closed by blankets and plastic!

Winter came early enough that we had to close in part of the basement with big sheets of plastic. (If this were a movie, at this point the music would change. You would know that what was to happen next would have great and unhappy impact on the lives of the players.) It was December, and John was working hard to finish closing in the house before more bad weather. He slipped and fell from a small ladder, bumping and bruising his midsection. He was showing the strain of eight months of building and still doing all his normal work on the job with his clients. Building the house, however, was a joy for him. It was how he defined relaxing. When his mother told him he was working too hard, he just replied, "Don't worry, Mom, I know what I'm doing."

Earlier that autumn John had made an exchange with a local farmer who grew wheat. John traded him some of our honey for some wheat because he was hungry for some good, homemade whole wheat bread. We had a stone grinder. The girls and I ground the grain and I made him the bread. He loved it and kept asking for more. But in February 1982 he turned down a piece fresh from the oven, still steaming and with butter melting on contact. He said it felt like he couldn't swallow it. And he began to talk about an ache in his stomach area. He thought that by this time the bruising from the ladder fall should have been gone.

When he went to his old family doctor I knew that he was in pain. Except for an appendectomy and the wounds from Vietnam, John and doctors were strangers. He was never sick. Examination showed nothing out of the ordinary. The doctor told him he was probably working too hard and was experiencing the results of too much stress. He reminded John that he had gone through a lot in the past three years. Perhaps he was expecting too much of himself. John agreed to take things a bit easier.

However, the discomfort persisted. John ignored as much of it as he could, continuing to roam the county meeting with his clients and working on the house every spare moment. I was the Chief Gopher. I can't even count the number of times I moved the same pile of two-by-fours from one side of the basement to the other. He even let me pound a few nails, but only in places that wouldn't show. He didn't like the dents I made when I would miss the head of the nail.

By May, even bicarbonate of soda was becoming less effective to settle his stomach, and eating was becoming a chore. The pain was not consistent, but it was there enough to be worrisome. John began to suspect he had an ulcer. He went back to his doctor, who this time took a series of upper gastrointestinal X rays. Nothing out of the ordinary showed on the film.

Early in June, John and I and the four girls took what would be our last real vacation. We called it our "UP" trip. We loaded up the van and headed southeast to St. Louis where we went UP into the Arch. Then we headed further east to the Outer Banks off North Carolina where we went UP the Cape Hatteras Light-house. We made our way north along the coast stopping at Kitty Hawk, Jamestown, Mt. Vernon, and finally Washington, D.C. We showed Sharon where she had been born at Fort Belvoir. I showed them all where I had lived in Annandale, and John showed us where he had lived there too. One last time we went UP, this time in the Washington Monument. During the trip eating became increasingly difficult for John. He didn't complain, and the girls were not aware anything was amiss.

When we arrived home, John decided he had better

see the doctor again. John's niece, a nurse, suggested that he see an internist at the clinic where she worked in Ames instead of the old family doctor. John agreed. It was now early July. Several different possible diagnoses were explained to John. Those X rays taken in May were read again. This new doctor gave John some stomach medication, suggested he stay away from certain foods, and told him to raise the head end of our bed four inches so that he would not be lying flat. He also suggested that if things didn't improve in the next couple of weeks John might want to consider a gastroscopy.

A gastroscope is a device with a fiberoptic end on a long tube that, when swallowed and inserted into the stomach, allows the surgeon to see what is there. This tube also allows insertion of a device for taking a biopsy of the stomach tissue. It didn't sound particularly pleasant.

John followed the doctor's instructions faithfully and did see some improvement. But one day in mid-August when he was in the courthouse in Boone, the pain in his stomach was so severe he rode the elevator to the third-floor courtroom instead of taking the stairs as he usually did.

Up to that point no one had mentioned cancer. Afterward people told me they had thought about that possibility but had dismissed it. After all, John was just thirty-eight years old. Thirty-eight-year-old healthy American men don't get stomach cancer. John had lost some weight and he did, on occasion, look a bit tired and even haggard. But building a house and working a job could easily have been responsible. The day in the courthouse, however, could not be ignored.

John went back to McFarland Clinic, and arrangements were made for the gastroscopy. On the morning of Friday, August 20, 1982, in the short stay unit of Mary Greeley Medical Center, the procedure was done. When Dr. Hardy, the surgeon, walked into the room, we both knew his news was bad. He told us he had seen a sizeable mass near the top of John's stomach where the esophagus joins it. He had removed some tissue to make sure, but even without the biopsy results, he said he was 85 to 90 percent sure it was a malignant tumor. He told us he would call us the next morning to let us know for sure.

The room was quiet as the four of us faced that truth. John and I, Dr. Hardy, and the nurse who had assisted him were somber. John asked questions. Dr. Hardy answered them clearly. He presented options. We were all calm. There were no tears, no hysterics, no angry words, just a calm acceptance. I know now that shocking news often brings that response. It is as if the mind hears but doesn't register information with its usual speed, seemingly working in slow motion. All other parts of the body go on as usual, but the word processor in the brain slows almost to a stop.

I had been reading a book while John was in the operating room. It was a spy thriller. In it an operative who knew he was terminally ill with cancer took on a particularly difficult assignment because he knew he was dying anyway. I set the book aside and couldn't read on. Cancer in a book was much easier to deal with than cancer in my husband. I could tell myself what was in the book wasn't real. But neither John nor I had that option with his body.

We left the short stay unit and drove to Boone to meet Dean and Helen. We had to sign one more document to clear the way for transferring our several high-interest home-improvement loans to a lower interest Federal Land Bank loan. I had finished painting the house on August 4, completing it on the outside. The Federal Land Bank demanded that and also clear and certain water rights. The spring that supplied the whole farm with water was on Dean's portion. A water easement agreement giving us permanent access to the water at its source would satisfy the Land Bank. The four of us met at the bank, had our signatures witnessed, and we told Dean and Helen what the doctor had said.

I don't remember much more of that day. I do remember the next morning, Saturday, August 21. John's girls were with us for the weekend. Dr. Hardy called as he had promised and confirmed his words of the day before. The biopsy showed carcinoma of the stomach. He and John talked about what step to take next. A surgery date was set five days hence, August 26, to attempt to remove the affected part of John's stomach.

We were to check in at Dr. Hardy's office on Monday.
We told the girls what was happening, and John and I
worked at being optimistic.

John went ahead with his scheduled bridge game
that evening. John, Keith, another cousin, Doug
Carlson, and a rotating fourth often played bridge on
weekend evenings. John saw no reason to upset that
routine now. But I found myself unsettled that night.
The men were playing bridge at our house; the girls
were settled in with things to do. I needed to talk, so I
called Judy. She was happy to go for a walk with me. As
we walked up the timber road, Judy let me ramble. She
told me then that I could call her at any time of the day
or night. She would be there. A time would come when
I would do that.

That was the beginning of a fifteen-month ordeal
through which John and I would walk together. At the
end of it would come the day he breathed for the last
time and I would be left alone. All those things we had
planned playfully to do when I got to be seventy and
he still the youngster of sixty-two would not happen.

In those fifteen months our hopes would soar when
a test showed good results, only to fall to earth when
the chemotherapy wasn't working after all. On the day
Dr. Hardy called with his confirmation of doom, we
didn't know the role that God would play in our two
lives. We didn't know about moments of grace. We
didn't know that what sounded to us as the end of
things was only the beginning pains of labor in our

spiritual birth process. We didn't know a living Lord who had been there before us and who would now walk us through our own *via dolorosa,* our own way of sorrows. We had no idea.

Later on in this story you will meet still more special people who walked with us on this journey. You will struggle along with me as I found the things God had in store for me. One of the earliest lessons we learned was that cancer has many faces and each person has his or her own experience.

For John, the battle with cancer was severe. First there was the attempt to remove the cancer surgically. This failed. Then, beginning in mid-September 1982, there were four and a half months of chemotherapy, complicated by pneumonia and devastating side effects that meant numerous hospitalizations. There was a ray of hope in February 1983 from a second gastroscopy. This hope was dashed in March with signs of new tumor growth. In April John had to stop working and go on disability. May saw him again in surgery, this time strictly palliative, to relieve suffering. From February on he needed regular blood transfusions. In August there was an attempt at an experimental chemotherapy protocol. This, too, was unsuccessful.

We spent every major holiday from Thanksgiving 1982 through Easter 1983 in the hospital. That is where we spent our third anniversary on Valentine's Day. That day, John needed blood. Finally on September 12

John entered the hospital for his final stay, the one that ended with his death on November 8.

John's oncologist assured us that only about 10 percent of cancer patients die excruciatingly painful deaths. John was a member of that select fraternity. Those last two months, despite liberal and innovative pain control therapy, he was never completely free of pain.

God in his graciousness allowed me to be present when John died. At least that time was beautifully peaceful. He was ready for the change that death would bring. He had asked his doctors to help speed the process. He had asked for extra life-support measures to be removed. He had said the good-byes he needed to say and had placed himself in God's hands. He had found victory in his ordeal of suffering, and I had been allowed to walk beside him through it all.

F O U R

God Began His Work

JOHN HAD KNOWN that the initial surgery had failed when he awoke and found himself in his own room in the hospital rather than in the intensive care unit. Those first few days of the battle had been sober ones. He began to think about death and was surprised to find that it wasn't the same as it had been—daily—in Vietnam. His symbol for death became leaving the girls. The promise he had made to himself when he was divorced, that he would not leave the girls no matter what, took on new meaning. Now he was having to face the possibility that he would not be able to keep his word.

As John was recovering from the surgery, I began what would become an oft-repeated pattern. I would stop in at the hospital to see him on my way to work, come back at lunchtime, and then again after work. Each evening as I left we would go through the same routine. "Call me when you get home," he would say.

He couldn't settle down for the night until he was sure I was safe at home.

One night that first week when I called to report my safe arrival I didn't sense anything unusual. But the next morning when I returned to his room he clung to me in tears. He told me that after I had left the night before he began to think about leaving the girls. He was overwhelmed by an enormous sadness. He wept for hours. And then something happened to him that he had never experienced before and didn't expect. The presence of God filled that hospital room and his life.

John told my brother on the phone a few days later, "R.C., there's something I have to tell you. Something happened to me in the hospital. For the first time in my life I sensed the presence of God and I just wanted to tell you. I don't know how this is going to work out, but no matter what happens, nobody can take that away from me." As he was confronting death, John was learning about life. The Quality he had been searching for was now defined: it was God. A God who broke into his life when he least expected it.

My own encounter with God forced its way into my consciousness eight months later. I was at Mary Greeley waiting for John's return to his room after surgery. It was quiet and I was alone. I had been pondering the meaning of our struggle and was thinking about how things are not always what they seem to be.

Buildings and people often have facades—faces for others to see that mask realities behind.

I began to write in free verse, trying to capture the essence. And then I knew—I had been in my own "far country," squandering my inheritance. God had been calling me, telling me that I was wanted at home. That call, though faint at first, was now loud and persistent. I began to see that the drama of my time with John was an analogy of God's caring. John loved me, not for what I had done but because he chose me. John accepted me because he wanted to, not because I had earned it.

That is the message God had for me. He, too, graciously wanted me with him, and he pursued me, just as John had. I had learned to spot those signs. God had drawn me into the fellowship of his people. He was carefully, inexorably leading me exactly where he wanted me to go. He was showing me that what I had once thought was so freeing was not. It was shoddy, cheap. Yet around me at this time was pain and suffering. I had always thought that those were to be avoided. God was showing me that I was wrong. He pointed me to his Son. I began to understand.

Two years before he became ill John had written a poem for me called "The Man in the Swamp." I was touched at the time. In it he spoke of his quest and his fearless approach to problems. Cancer changed that, at least on the outside. The man dying in Room 271 at

MGMC was no longer the "tough, alert, tall, immune to many dangers" person in the swamp. He wasn't pretty to look at anymore, but he *was* victorious. As he died by inches he was slowly stripped of every way he knew of how to define living. Once able to attempt virtually any task, now he could do nothing more than sit in a chair. Yet for each ability that was taken away, he was given grace to minister to those of us around him. As he was dying, he kept on giving to anyone who was unafraid to be with him. When we couldn't give to him, he gave to us. When we couldn't love him, he loved us. You see, he had nothing to lose.

One of the nurses who cared for him wrote at his funeral:

> As a nurse, when I'd come on duty and see him for the first time that day, he would greet me with such understanding. Words were never necessary. He would reach out for a hug, pat me on the back, and say, "I know, I know." He really did know. *He* was comforting *me.*

John learned the secret of life—when it is no longer possible to hold on to it, it is OK to let go. The surprise is that what you get in return is life!

Does that sound familiar? Didn't our Lord say that those who would save their lives would lose them, and that those who were willing to lose their lives would find them? I actually watched that happen with John.

But some people around John missed seeing this happen. Their own fear and dis-ease made John's diseased state repugnant to them. They couldn't see past the exterior, and some of them still can't. In more than a year's worth of widow-days, I have found that it is very difficult for many people to talk about death. They would simply rather not. I don't know if it is too frightening, a message of their own mortality that they don't want to face, or just too uncomfortable to deal with. In my grief I wanted to talk about death, about John, about all the good things and all the bad things. I wanted to examine them inside and out to see what was there. I have no idea if I will have the grace to die as courageously as John did. I saw him victorious, though, and I don't want others to miss that. There is comfort there for me and for them.

Death is an easy thing to deny—sometimes easier to deny than to accept. For example, my brother-in-law Dean said that it seems to him that John is just away for a while and that he'll be back. Then everything will be OK. But that is not true.

John's daughters have had a difficult time expressing anything about his death. We continue the routine we had when he was still alive. The girls spend every other weekend with me at my house. Their mother has remarried and they are part of two families. But it became clear to me about five months after John's death that they were pretending that things were like they had been and that everything would just go on. We would do all the things we had done before—only without John.

I found myself deeply resenting this bizarre situation. Here were these girls making demands on me and John was not even here anymore. One day I became very angry at the girls. (It is easy to get angry at people when the situation is at fault.) I am not proud of that. I felt it was important to let them know that I love them while getting across to them that things would never again be the way they were.

It is hard to say to children, "Your father is dead." But it is a mistake, I feel, not to address the reality. Death changes the living. I have been forced to confront conflicting feelings about responsibilities to a situation that no longer exists (the blended family John and I had) and the realization that I must carve out a new life for myself without him. I have learned that I cannot hold on to what no longer exists.

My awareness of grief in others has been significantly heightened. I noticed many more people who had losses than I had ever noticed before. One such was Alice. She arrived for her appointment with me in her nurse's whites. She looked pleasant and acted pleasantly. She had come to talk with me about family finances. As I wrote the intake information, I began to get a picture of a woman overwhelmed by loss and deep into grief. She and Tom have three children, all adopted. She told me the first one (now age eight) cost $1,500, the second (now age three) cost $4,000, and the third (now eight months old) had cost them $7,000 earlier this year because of severe complications at

birth. Family finances were tight! They welcomed
these children but did not like going into debt for court
and adoption fees. Alice's nursing is part-time in the
Intensive Coronary Care Unit (ICCU). At best, hers is
a stressful job.

As she talked on I learned that three weeks after
their second child was adopted, her mother had a
massive coronary and died. Alice was devastated but
didn't really take time to grieve since she had a brand-
new baby to care for. Before long her dad remarried—
a woman Alice's age! Alice had attempted to secure
prenuptial agreements, but her father assured her that
Cheryl was "not that kind of person." Three months
after Alice and Tom adopted their youngest baby, they
learned that Alice's dad had cancer with a poor prog-
nosis. Another blow! Two months later while on duty
in the ICCU Alice got a call from a neighboring hospital
to prepare for a sixty-four-year-old male: massive
coronary, needs ventilator machine, arriving within
twenty minutes. Name: Robert Wilson—Alice's dad.
She held on, got the equipment ready, and then told
her supervisor, "That's my father who is coming."
When her shift was over she sat with her dad. She was
the only family with him when he died two hours later.

Alice and her sister were named executrixes of the
estate. Cheryl turned out to be "that kind of person,"
refused to pay for the $5,000 funeral, took all the
insurance benefits, and petitioned the estate (and won)
a $500 per month widow's allowance for a year. In a

depressed housing market where eight hundred homes were for sale in a town of twelve thousand, Alice and her sister had to sell their dad's house for a significant loss in order to pay Cheryl. Six months after his death, Alice was *angry*. She realized she hadn't mourned for him, nor for her mom who died three years earlier. And her communication with Tom hadn't been too good lately.

Because of my own grief, I could touch Alice. I told her in a few words about John to establish a link between us. We talked at length about loss and grief. I was both pleased and surprised that I was able to see and identify some of her feelings because I had known them intimately myself.

I gave Alice an assignment. I asked her to write a letter to her dad telling him how angry she was at him for leaving her and how she felt about his remarrying after her mom died. I suggested she read it to him as if he were there.

Two visits later Alice brought in her letter. She had really let him have it! She told him she knew she had been his favorite and that she wanted so much his forgiveness and to be able to forgive him. I was very moved when I'd finished reading. When I looked up, she was quietly watching me. "I cried, Bobbie," she said. "I really cried. Tom took me to the cemetery and I cried again. Now, maybe, I'm beginning to work this through." She thanked me for suggesting she write the letter.

Alice had been "seeing" her dad in different places—
out in the garden, walking on the street. She was
shocked and frightened by these hallucinations. She
seemed relieved when I told her I had experienced that
with John, and that books I had read said it was a
normal and usual occurrence. She thought she was
losing her mind. Grief is such a lonely thing. Sometimes strange things happen, and since people do not
often talk about them, they never learn that others
have those same feelings and experiences.

During one visit Alice told me about a man of fifty in
the ICCU with congestive heart failure. He had been
particularly irritable that day on her shift. She told me
that when she became more in touch with her own
fears, she was able to be in touch with his. She went
over, sat down on the bed, took his hands in hers and
asked, "Mr. ———, are you afraid you are going to die
in here?" With that simple query, he was released from
his solitary confinement. They talked about his wife
and family and preparations for death, each giving
solace to the other.

I was surprised to find shortly after John's death how
much of my energy for all those months of his illness
had been spent just coping with the mechanics of that
illness. Now, not only was he gone, but also gone were
those daily trips to the hospital and nightly calls to
family members to keep them informed. I had a rest-
lessness I wasn't expecting and a hunger to talk with
others who had undergone a similar loss. I began

searching for a widows' support group. I found one seventy miles away. Michael, a young man of thirty who had been widowed six months previously, offered to drive with me to Grinnell for the meeting.

The weather had been bad all winter, and I was glad to have someone to go to the meeting with and also not to have to drive on the ice. It took us almost two hours to get to Grinnell. Michael and I had time to get acquainted. He expressed anger at his situation. Here he was, left with two young children, his dreams shattered, and nothing to look forward to. He was having difficulty keeping his job and caring for his kids. I was surprised at the bitterness Michael was expressing at his wife for dying.

I realized then that having some time of knowing that death is imminent has benefits both for the person dying and for those left behind. John and I had been given time to think and talk about what it would be like after his death. We could share some of the grief in preparation of his dying and we could dissipate some of the anger. Michael never had a chance to do that. Instead, just when he and his wife thought everything was going to be all right, that the scare had passed, she died suddenly. He learned then one of the cruelest lessons of widowhood—when a person dies, everyone in that person's life crosses a line. There is no going back. It is no longer the way it was.

The aspect of Michael's anger that I had difficulty understanding was the part that was directed

against his wife. I had not experienced that. I was mad
at the circumstances I was having to deal with, and
somewhat mad at John for leaving me to cope without
him, but I never felt the kind of anger toward John that
Michael was expressing toward his wife. It was almost
as if he needed her back to settle a few things before he
could go on.

John had spent his last few days saying good-bye to
special people—his brother, sisters, mother, cousins,
nieces, in-laws, friends, and colleagues. The last time
he saw the girls was probably the hardest. His fear that
he would have to leave them (which he had mourned
that night fifteen months earlier) was now becoming a
reality. We all gathered in Room 271 as a blended
family. John told the girls they were the three best girls
a father could ever have had. My daughter pouted. I
caught his eye and directed it over to her. He smiled
and amended his comment, "The best three and a half
daughters. . . ." She beamed with that acceptance. He
made sure they knew he didn't want to leave them and
told them he loved them very much.

The girls never saw his tears, nor did his brother and
sisters. He waited each time until the other people left
before he allowed his own grief to be expressed. That
was for me alone to witness and share.

John never said good-bye to me. Twice in those last
few days he held me close and whispered, "I don't want
to leave you." That was it: "I don't want to leave you."

I did find a local group to meet with to discuss loss.

This small group was facilitated by a woman who was an elementary school counselor. The other members of the group, two men and two women, had experienced their losses through divorce. They were kind and solicitous toward me, but when I spoke of death it was too much for them. One of the women even vocalized it: "I don't know how you do it. Death—I couldn't handle that." As she said that, she even backed away from me physically.

I thought of the irony I was experiencing, even here in a group expressly designed for dealing with loss. When I spoke of mine, the group's reaction was that it was too much to deal with. Divorce apparently was a safe topic; death, too terrible to think about. I was reminded that the sorority/fraternity of bereavement to which I now belonged was a select one indeed, but one that no one petitioned to join.

Nevertheless, even that evening was a moment of grace. Those people did not shut me out, nor did they force me into silence. Knowing that what they would hear would not be pleasant, still they allowed me to talk of my loss and deal with its realities. Death frightens all of us. Being with the grieving takes courage and discipline. It is much easier to say (or think), "Oh, I'm sorry," and then do nothing.

The Bible speaks often of the needs of widows and orphans, and directs people toward meeting them. I think I know why. If I were not urged, urged, and then urged again, I don't think I'd purposefully put myself into such painful situations. Listening to a grieving person takes energy. And, then, when I want to be able to make everything all right, I realize I can't. Sometimes there is nothing I can do but listen. Often, of course, nothing more is being asked.

The deep needs of people in grief require much comfort, patience, and companionship. Some people's attempts to provide spiritual perspective amount to nothing more than pious-sounding pat answers. For example, shortly after John's death our Sunday school class was discussing prayer. A woman well into her eighties was giving a testimony to the power of prayer in her life by telling how her husband had recovered from an illness in response to her prayers. I told her that fervent prayer does not always result in physical healing. John was a case in point: People across the country had prayed for him, yet he died of cancer. She looked at me with a special knowing look that said, "Well, you obviously didn't have enough faith."

Once again it became painfully obvious to me that I needed more food for my spiritual hunger. My needs were not being met in that little country church. Judy Carlson and I decided to find a church with evening services we could attend. Judy and Keith, throughout John's illness and beyond, have been a continuing moment of grace. Stable, caring friends are what every widowed person needs. Without Judy I doubt I would have had the strength to break the routine of going to the country church and coming home angry and unfed.

We found our evening service, and I found a continuing community of caring. I met Donna Barker that first evening. She greeted us each time we came. One night I asked her if there was a group in the church for people dealing with loss. She said no, but a few days later she phoned and invited me out to lunch. From that grew our discipling friendship. Our time together has known a number of moments of grace. She knew I needed to be put to work, so she asked me to consider membership on a church committee. She also asked me to help her put together the Sunday morning bulletins. These were specific, concrete ways that I could be doing something. Without them I might have continued simply to exist in my grief, unable to take an active role in my own life.

I wanted to join the church but wasn't sure if I would fit in. I spoke with the pastor about some of my concerns. He wisely told me not to worry. "Let us minister to you here, Bobbie. Let us help you heal. Your ministry is in your job. You do that. We'll give you comfort here." So the church became a sanctuary, a place of refuge where it was safe for me to take those hesitant first steps back among the living.

I learned later that people in the church's Wednesday evening prayer group had been praying for both John and me, without even knowing us, during his illness. A

former coworker of mine had prayed for us when she
learned of John's illness. "What an engineer God is!"
Donna wrote to me. So many times during the last two
and a half years I have seen God's hand at work.

I continued my search for another "widows' group"
closer to home. Eight months after John died I still felt
a need to check my experiences with others in similar
situations, but I was beginning to wonder if I was too
far removed from the event. I had read every book I
could find and had already learned important lessons.
But I had never really spent time exploring with
another person what it was like to be widowed.

I finally found a local group. It, too, was a small
group limited to those who had lost someone close—
spouse, child, parent. It was facilitated by a woman
working in hospice and by a local minister. Except for a
woman who had lost her thirteen-year-old son, I was
the youngest person present. As people told why they
were there, I found my heart going out to women who
spoke of thirty, thirty-five, and forty years with their
husbands prior to bereavement. The loneliness they
were expressing, not in words but in looks, tone of
voice, and disbelief, was all too real. That night I heard
anger—and bewilderment, hopelessness, despair. I
heard very little hope, and I began to take the role of
hope-giver.

That evening was a moment of grace—an unexpected one, surely, but one nonetheless. I began to see
concretely that healing was happening in me, and I

really began to hope that it would happen in these women as well. Healing in a group context, however, demands a certain willingness to risk shared feelings. Not all the women were able to be that vulnerable, and several dropped out. The group was left too small to continue, so the isolation continued for us all.

Statistics show that three-quarters of married persons become widows or widowers at some point, and this stands to reason. Yet our families, institutions, and schools do so little to prepare us for that event. Each of us is left alone, hoping it won't happen to us and putting off any preparation. When bereavement occurs, we find ourselves nearly immobilized, wondering *how, why, when, who*—and unable even to finish the questions. Moments of grace, seeing God's hand at work, have given me encouragement and hope in my times of deepest need.

F I V E
God Will Provide

A WOMAN walked up to me at church after the Sunday evening service. She looked familiar, but I couldn't put a name to her. "Hi, I'm Marilyn from Grinnell. I met you a year ago." Of course! Marilyn had been responsible for inviting me to that widows' group in Grinnell and had arranged my transportation with Michael.

We had much to talk about, including what I had learned in my first year of being a widow. I mentioned that I hadn't met many men who had been widowed and that I still had few insights into their coping with the problems. "Here's one," she said, and introduced me to Bob.

Bob said he and Marilyn were completing a double date begun twenty-six years ago. His wife had been Marilyn's good friend, and the two families had kept in touch over the years by exchanging Christmas letters between Iowa and Wisconsin. Bob's wife died of cancer. He took some time for healing. Marilyn had been a widow for fifteen years. And, now, here they were together. Both felt that God had planned their relationship and had provided each for the other. I asked Bob about that and he pointed me to the Bible:

> *You have sent troubles and suffering on me,*
> *but you will restore my strength;*
> *you will keep me from the grave.*
> *You will make me greater than ever;*
> *you will comfort me again.* PSALM 71:20-21

> *Find a wife and you find a good thing;*
> *it shows that the Lord is good to you.* PROVERBS 18:22

Bob said that this "find" was not an "out-searching" for him. But when God places an opportunity before you, you take it. He went on, "After my wife died, the first book I turned to was the Psalms. I found things that I had never seen there before!"

While Bob and Marilyn were talking, inside I was hearing, "Bobbie, remember, you don't have to worry about how I will provide for you. All you have to do is remember to trust that I will provide. Haven't I promised to be with you?" God, through the lives of real people who had been where I am now, was reminding me, in the only way I seem to learn, that he is faithful.

I had learned during John's illness that the question to ask was not *why* but *who*. He wasn't getting better. Nothing seemed to be working. He kept on dying by inches. Yet, as he died, we both grew.

Well into John's illness we were given Harold Kushner's book *When Bad Things Happen to Good People*.
Kushner wrote at length about Job. I went back to the
Scriptures and read for myself. When I came to the
part where God questions Job I began to get a glimmer.
With each of those queries I questioned *myself* more
and more. *Who am I even to place such a question as
why to God?* And then I found the gem:

> *I know, Lord, that you are all-powerful;*
>   *that you can do everything you want.*
> *You ask how I dare question your wisdom*
>   *when I am so very ignorant.*
> *I talked about things I did not understand,*
>   *about marvels too great for me to know.*
> *You told me to listen while you spoke*
>   *and to try to answer your questions.*
> **Then I knew only what others had told me,**
>   **but now I have seen you with my own eyes.**
> *So I am ashamed of all I have said*
>   *and repent in dust and ashes.* JOB 42:2-6 (emphasis added)

I understand what that means in my life. It was an
extremely difficult and painful lesson to learn. It cost
me my "pearl of great price"—John, my husband,
because I learned it through his death. To know *about*
God isn't enough. I had to learn to *know* God, the
sovereign One, outside of whom *nothing* happens.
Once that became real to me, I understood that as long
as I asked *why* I would never get an answer I could live
with. But the answer to *who*—God—is able to satisfy,

heal, sustain, give me life. John and I talked about that together. That is why a central part of his funeral service was directed toward that idea.

However, my learning had just begun. Though I had satisfied not *why*—but *who,* and was understanding more about the sovereignty of God, I wasn't sure how he would care for me. This struggle would go on for a year before I could put into words what I was experiencing. Marilyn and Bob became the personification of the question. The essence of the struggle for me was one of control. I like things planned and ordered. I like to know when, how, what. I like to *decide* when, how, what. John and I watched what little control we had disappear during his illness.

I have had to learn to live in a world that I cannot control. The weather doesn't get my permission to happen. Iowa winters can be severe. Snowdrifts that block all exit from my home in the country don't ask me if it is all right for them to be there. The mechanical things around the house simply don't understand that I have "machine anxiety" and that John had been their keeper. They malfunction when they please. And my widow's car does not miraculously no longer need its oil changed and its engine maintained.

This particular issue of control has been addressed in "I Can Cope," a series of seminars held at our medical center sponsored by the American Cancer Society for cancer patients and their families. We heard it stated simply there:

Learn to control everything that is subject to your control.
Forget what is beyond your control.

How easy that is to say! I can even do it—for five
minutes, maybe, once a month. It is far easier for this
widow to come home from work in the evening, tired
like everyone else after a long day of listening to
people, and do nothing, except perhaps sit in the living
room and feel sorry for herself. That isn't what "control
everything that is subject to your control" means. That
is letting what I can control, control me. And the other
side of that behavior is the one where I just go and go
and do and do to prove I'm not just vegetating, that I'm
not feeling sorry for myself.

That is not the message God has given us as his
children. That kind of lethargy or busyness are really
saying that I am still worrying about *how*. When I learn
to approach my life with a healthy attitude I discover
that Dean means it when he tells me that he'll keep the
snow plowed out of my driveway. And Jerry, my own
private "Japanese technician" (and dear friend), will
keep an eye on my Japanese car. And Keith will help
me winterize the doors, ripping the boards and sawing
them to their proper size. It means it is all right for me
to ask others to help me do those things I cannot do for
myself.

I don't have to learn to do all the things John did in
our life together, but I do have to learn where to go to
find the proper someone to do the job. That seems to

me to be taking control in areas where I can. "Forgetting what is beyond my control" doesn't mean, I have discovered, giving up hopes and dreams of contentment, happiness, and a full life. What it does mean is that my trust that God is in control must be an active one. I must practice believing that God means it when he promises to provide.

Anticipating the second Christmas after John died proved to be difficult. I didn't have any extra money, so buying presents for five children became a challenge. I began to look for ways to be creative and to find extra resources. For a little over a year John's tools had sat idle in his shop in the basement. The radial arm saw, table saw, planer, drill press, and the others were beginning to show signs of disuse. Perhaps, I told myself, I could begin to part with them, to place them where they could be used. I cleaned them up, put on a coat of protective lubricant to halt rusting, and advertised them for sale.

The wood/coal-burning stove in our living room that saved us so much on our propane bill and was so cozy to sit by on cold Iowa nights hadn't been used since John's last hospitalization. Somehow the rustic glamour—splitting wood with the "John Carlson Special" log splitter, hauling it in, feeding the stove, watching that it didn't get too hot, carrying out the ashes, and every now and then making a trip up on the roof to be a chimney sweep—was gone without him. My single life-style did not really need these

things. I began to plan to find new homes for the tools
and stove. Perhaps that would make Christmas gifts a
possibility.

Then one day the week before Christmas the mail
brought me two Christmas cards. One was from a new
friend, a fellow alto from the church choir. The other
had a typewritten address, no return address, and a
local postmark—not much in the way of clues. It was
the same card as the one from my friend. Its message
was a hope that this Christmas and the new year ahead
would bring a new appreciation and awareness of
God's special love and care for me. The card was
unsigned. In it, neatly folded, was a bank draft for a
hundred dollars! I didn't know what to do so I went
into the living room and sat down and cried.

I know that this was God's provision for me. I was
overwhelmed. How surprised I was, and how quickly I
realized that I didn't believe God really would provide.
Gift-buying for the children was easier. Then Keith told
me he had a buyer for one of the saws! And Jerry
wanted another one of them. His down payment was a
good checkup on my car. Within a month all five of the
major tools were in new shops, bringing joy to other
workers of wood.

When the last of them was sold, I laid the check on
the dining room table, saw the people out, came back
and looked at the check again, and felt an awful,
terrible hole right in the middle of me. I didn't understand. Money had been so tight and here was a break. I

stared at the check. It was as if I had betrayed John. I went into the living room, sat down in my chair, and cried again. That night as I wrote my prayers, this is what I told God:

> Once again you have shown me in reality that you mean it when you say you will provide. Thank you for the tools being sold. I have a sadness, though, because I know how much they meant to John. Perhaps that's why I've felt so sad these past few days—selling the tools removes him from my life. He really is gone. That shop was a symbol of him. I've been fooling myself for a year, Father. He is gone.

Three days before Christmas the youth pastor at the church called and asked if he could come out. He brought a gift from the congregation—a turkey, other food, and fifty dollars from my "Family at E. Free." This time I really didn't know what to do. I certainly didn't perceive myself as needy! But I was! My budget didn't leave room for many extras. Here was an opportunity for me to be generous to others.

It has been hard at times to be the receiver of so much from so many. I have been humbled. I know others will stand where I am now and I will have the chance to help in God's provision for them. But receiving this kind of abundance has been a sobering lesson in the graciousness and mercy of God. I have learned again what it means to be beholden. And God doesn't want things back from me. All he wants is me, all of me. I think I am beginning to understand that he does mean it when he says he will provide and that what he has in store for me will be special. Not only that, but his plans will be what I most desire. He will see to it that his plans and my desires become one and the same, most probably by working in me to change my desires to what he wants for me.

Nonetheless, the lesson is sure. I don't need to ask *why,* because now I know *who.* Nor do I need to wonder *how;* I will trust that *God will provide.*

Loneliness

I THINK one of the reasons the house seemed so lonely the night after John's funeral was that the contrast with the preceding two days was so great. There had been so many things to do to get ready, and people made sure I wasn't alone. But obviously, the time had to come when they would go home and I would have the house to myself.

I had spent the previous two months in exactly the same way—alone, by myself in the house. But this night was different because I knew when I woke up the next day I wouldn't be going to the hospital to see John. I wouldn't even be going to the funeral home. In fact, I wouldn't need to go anywhere or do anything. It was all over. I could stop the hectic pace now, stop and let emotions that had been put on hold have their hour.

Strangely enough, what I began to think about was how much I had to tell John about—all the things the people said, how wonderful the nurses had been, Dr. Zaentz and Dr. Hardy and. . . . But there wasn't any

John to tell, and there never would be again. It was over.

Now nothing remained to be done but to go through his things and take care of all the paperwork for insurance claims, veteran and social security forms, credit cards, and the like. I decided to take care of his clothes and personal effects right away. I knew I had to change just a few things to keep myself aware that he wasn't coming back. Going through his clothes and papers wasn't too hard. I even made it through all the problems of paying the hospitals and doctors. But the workshop in the basement was another matter.

John's last project before he went into the hospital the last time had been building a deck and stairs inside the front door in the new part of our house. When able, John had continued to work at finishing the inside. The floor of the basement was three and a half feet below outside ground level. The deck and stairs made it possible to remove the combination of wooden steps and concrete blocks that had masqueraded as the entryway for so long.

John loved wood and enjoyed creating with it. He was a careful craftsman. Each time I look at the deck I am overwhelmed by the pain he was in when he worked that wood. Every nail is a mute testimony to his courage. He made the deck out of redwood that he planed down from rough-cut boards and fitted together. It was all finished except the top and side railings.

One Saturday in mid-December 1983 John's girls
and I were decorating the living room. My niece Terry
came over. I was in the midst of tinsel and Christmas
lights. Terry stepped over a few and sat down in the
living room. Earlier that day Jerry had asked if he
could use the radial arm saw. As Terry and I were
talking, I forgot Jerry was downstairs working on one
of the railings for the deck. I heard the saw start its
awful whine and thought, *John's at it again. Maybe he'll
get the deck done today and I can work on putting on the
finish over the holidays.* Just as quickly, that thought
stopped and another took its place. *That isn't John down
there. He's dead. That's Jerry using the saw.* I must have
had a funny look on my face because Terry asked me
what was wrong. I told her through a few tears, and
then we went on with our conversation, because going
on is all there is to do.

I missed him. I just plain missed him. He wasn't
there to smile at me, encourage me, share with me
what happened in his day, love me, hold me. Nor was
he there for me to give him all those Christmas gifts as
we had done before.

I had begun earlier that year reading through the
Bible. I was in Isaiah. I was stunned to find this passage:

> *Do not be afraid—you will not be disgraced again;*
>   *you will not be humiliated.*
> *You will forget your unfaithfulness as a young wife,*
>   *and your desperate loneliness as a widow.*

Your Creator will be like a husband to you—
  the Lord Almighty is his name.
The holy God of Israel will save you—
  he is the ruler of all the world. ISAIAH 54:4-5

This was as accurate a reading of my life as I had ever seen. I had known that unfaithfulness as a young wife and now I was desperately lonely as a widow. God put those words there just for me. But God being a husband to me . . . I began to wonder what that meant.

Part of the struggle of learning to couple "life" and "widow" has been solving the mystery of what this means in real, everyday experience. How can my Creator be like a husband to me? Can he touch me, comfort me, hug me, tease me, fuss with me? Can he? I'd never had that happen. My way of understanding the secrets of God has always been through other people, and now, where was the one through whom I was learning about love? He was gone, and all I had left in his place were some words that told me my Creator would be like a husband to me.

I made an appointment to talk with the pastor of the First Evangelical Free Church. I had several things I wanted to talk about; one of them was loneliness. I was forty-seven years old, and there hadn't been a time in thirty-five of these years that there hadn't been some male who had captured my interest. Now that category was empty. No one, just memories. I spoke with the pastor about missing the closeness. I showed him the passage in Isaiah. "It is a comfort to know God is there caring for me, loving me, saving me as a husband," I told him, "but it's not quite the same."

He smiled and told me about an incident when his oldest daughter, Jodi, was small.

She had been tucked in one night with her favorite stuffed friends, but sleep was playing hard-to-get. She had already had the traditional drink of water and story. But they were ineffective. So Dad went up to comfort her. "Jodi, you're not alone. Here are all your friends with you to keep you company."

"But, Daddy," she wailed, "I need someone with blood!"

Oh boy, I knew exactly what she had meant as soon as I heard those words. That was what I was expressing: "I need someone with blood!" But there wasn't someone with blood, only a memory of a husband who had loved me, and some words on a page.

I have wrestled often with those words, and I gain something new each time I return to them. Perhaps part of it is because I found a companion piece, also in Isaiah:

> But the Lord says,
> "Do not cling to events of the past
>   or dwell on what happened long ago.
> Watch for the new thing I am going to do.
>   It is happening already—you can see it now!"
> ISAIAH 43:18-19

Slowly, ever so slowly over my first year as a widow I began to learn, to see what God was teaching me. I have begun to see that God is in charge and to believe that a new thing is happening. It had been very hard to imagine living without a husband, but with each day I realize I am doing just that.

That first year, every time I went down to the shop area in the basement, I looked at the wood scraps haphazardly lying along one wall. *I've got to straighten those up,* I told myself a hundred times. But I just kept walking by.

I had taken a six-month leave of absence from CCJ in October 1983 so I could be with John in the hospital. He died three weeks later, but I couldn't go back to work because a replacement had been hired for the whole six months. So I set some goals for myself for that time. One was to put the finish on the deck to protect the wood from wet and dirty feet. I walked past that a hundred times, too.

Finally, a month before I was to return to work, I did it—sanding and finishing, sanding and finishing. The redwood glowed as its inner beauty and grain were revealed. And I saw a parable of myself in that. In this moment of grace I saw that I was being sanded and finished, sanded and finished to bring out my inner beauty. Like the deck, I am not completed. It and I still lack the final railings.

The pile of wood scraps was another matter, however. It took a whole year before I straightened them

up. The inertia of loneliness is so difficult to overcome.
One Saturday morning near the first anniversary of
John's death I decided it was time. I spent several
hours sorting and piling and vacuuming and rearrang-
ing, and I got it done. At last the shop didn't look as if
its owner had just taken an iced tea and cookie break. I
felt good about it.

Sometimes the loneliness is awful. I literally ache to
be held close. Sometimes being alone is a blessed relief,
for I don't need to pretend I am doing so well and can
let down my guard.

I know I've got a place to go when I need to be with
people—a half mile down the road to Keith and Judy's.
(Keith and John had a special relationship as cousins.
John would often say to me, "I want to check out what
Keith thinks about this." He would then hop into the
blue van and head south. They did things together,
thought through things together, and loved each
other.) They have walked with me through every step
of John's illness, his death, and my aloneness. They
have given me an immeasurable gift. And they are not
doing this just because of John; I am their friend in my
own right.

The time came when I remembered Judy's offer to
call her at any time of the day or night, and I took her
at her word. John had had a particularly restless evening in the hospital. It was a few days after one of his
stomach surgeries. The medication he was given to
stop painful spasms did that, but it confused his mind

as well. He was convinced he was at home and kept
trying to get out of bed. That was dangerous because
he was attached to IV bottles connected to his Hickman
catheter. A Hickman is a permanent opening that has a
tube making direct access to a major vein. It is used for
giving medications, feeding, taking blood samples,
giving blood transfusions. When it is not in use, it is
kept securely clamped shut. John, always a fix-it man,
even in his confused state kept undoing the connection.
Every time that happened, he would begin to bleed
through the Hickman. That is what he was doing this
particular evening. He didn't know me or anyone else,
and he wouldn't stay in bed.

I went home about ten o'clock and the nurses assured me they would call if there was any trouble. At
3:00 A.M. the phone rang. It was John and he was
delirious. He kept telling me not to leave him. When
the nurse got on the phone, she explained that he was
convinced I wasn't coming back to see him. We decided
I'd better get back there in a hurry. They had tried
restraining John but could do so for only ten seconds. I
called Judy and asked if she would go to the hospital
with me. "I'll be ready in ten minutes," she said.

We were able to get John calmed down a little. By
then he recognized me and was assured I wasn't going
to leave him. Judy rested and I sat with John until six.
Then Judy came to take her turn and I rested. A little
later when I went back into the room John was climb-
ing all over his bed, the trapeze over his bed, off the

bed and onto a chair, stretching the tubing connected
to his Hickman to its limit. He saw some writing on the
curtain and was struggling to read it. Judy was marvel-
ous. She held the curtain so John could "read" it and
for a long time he read words only he could see, asking
her to move the drape here or pull it there as he followed the writing.

At about eight Dr. Zaentz came in. Without even
taking off his jacket he sat down on the bed, put his
arm around John and asked him what was going on.
He quieted John and then was able to find a medication
that worked to release John's mind from its turmoil. By
midafternoon he was himself again, chuckling with the
rest of us over reading the drape.

Judy is one of those special people who knows how
to listen. She has let me sputter, wonder, think, cry,
and plan, always keeping me focused on real matters.
She has fed me, walked with me, and most of all included me in special events. She and Keith have convinced me that I can be comfortable with them in my
singleness. That has not been easy. But with them I
know it is all right to be myself. I am learning to do
that slowly with other couples, but nowhere quite so
gracefully as with Keith and Judy.

Within a marriage there are many ways of expressing
intimacy—a look, a touch, a word, or long, quiet
conversations between just two nestled before a fire,
the sharing of special moments. And, of course, the
sexual act itself. For John and me, that was not a

possibility the last year of his life. Shortly after his death I remember wondering if I had completely shut down any kind of sensuality or feelings or desiring closeness. There was nothing there. I talked a lot about finding another man, having a date, even possibly marrying again. But it was only talk.

On one occasion at an all-day meeting in another city, a fellow committee member complimented me on my appearance. He told me I'd better be careful because I looked good enough to be kissed. There was invitation in his eyes and his voice. Inside me warning bells sounded. I found myself hungering for the attention and wanting more, and at the same time I almost panicked. I wanted to run away.

For days afterward I was unsettled. I began to wonder what I would do if anyone paid real attention to me as a woman, something more than this obviously flirtatious comment. I find I long for the intimacy I once knew and am terrified at the thought that it might just come along!

I've thought much about such a relationship. I've been advised by friends to get out where men are and enjoy myself, be "available." Some have even suggested that I should find creative ways to initiate such contacts. But I'm not doing those things for at least two reasons: One, that is not my style. Two, I don't think the time is right for me. There is still some healing that needs to take place. I would like to meet and be able to

interact socially with men on a nonthreatening level.
I'm not interested in affairs with either single or mar-
ried men. If John taught me nothing else, he taught me
I am worth far more than that!

Widows' books tell a person not to make any major
decisions for at least a year. I have found that good
advice. However, my brother suggested shortly after
John's funeral that perhaps it would help if I got a
permanent to curl my severely straight hair, bought
contacts to replace my glasses, and learned to use
cosmetics. There is no doubt that I was showing the
effects of a long and stressful fifteen months. He told
me these things in the context of a discussion on the
possibilities of remarriage, but I have found that by
doing these things I got a boost in my feelings about
myself. It has been fun to see the difference. For so
long all that was important was seeing that John was as
pain-free and comfortable as possible. This intense
concern took a toll on me, and the pampering I have
done for myself has lifted my spirits.

I find it far easier to talk about loneliness in the
abstract—on a day when the sun is shining, I am
feeling good, and there are no hard decisions to make.
It is just plain awful to talk about it in the midst of one
of those hard decisions.

A man asked me out to dinner! He would be in town
for a meeting and he thought it would be nice if I
would have dinner with him. *Oh yes,* I thought, *it*

would be more than nice. He said he would call me to
make final arrangements, but I should keep next
Tuesday open.

But it is not quite that easy. This is a man who has
already let me know he would like to have more than
dinner. I was able to tell him I wasn't interested in
being more than friends. I don't really know what he
thought about that. I know that I responded eagerly to
knowing I was still attractive to a male—and a charm-
ing one at that. But . . . *he is married, very married.* He
has chosen to stay that way and has found relationships
on the side. I had already told him I did not want to be
anybody's on-the-side relationship.

But what to do about dinner? I am strong enough (I
think) to keep such an occasion on a friendly basis. He
is definitely enough of a gentleman to respect that. But
what kind of signal am I sending him if I go? What
about my very definite vulnerability in this area? It has
been many months since I have been alone with a man
on a "date," and even that was with John. What I
struggle with has nothing to do with my friend. He will
probably stay my friend even after I tell him I won't go
out to dinner with him and why. No, the struggle is
within me. I am shocked at how much I *want* to go out
with him, at how pleasant it is to anticipate being with
a man. I want the attention I know he will show me
and the intimacy of an evening for two at a good
restaurant. I want the fun of it. None of these things are
wrong in themselves. But they are wrong with him

because he has a wife at home. He is not free to be with me that way, and I am not free to encourage that kind of unfaithfulness.

I am struggling not to be willful and disobedient to God. I am struggling with emotions that have lain dormant for a long time. I long for an eligible man to ask me out for that dinner. But I cannot go this time—not with this man. I would not be honest with him or myself if I did.

I find my attitude in this area is not yet settled. I am open both to the possibility of another good relationship with a man, maybe even marriage, and to the real possibility of being single from now on. I know I don't need a man to be complete, and I also know that with the right one marriage would be a great fulfillment for us both. A marriage now would include paying attention to God's standards, doing things his way, something I had not done before. I would know the joy of submitting both to what God would have me do and to a man who would love me with that sacrificial love modeled by Jesus.

Slowly my ability to empathize with others—to be able to enjoy a good love story or film without mourning my lack in that area—is coming back. I found myself beaming with pleasure as two nieces and a cousin were married this year and wishing for each of them the joys John and I shared. One of them, Deb, a lovely young woman, touched me deeply when she wrote:

I'm thankful you were brought into our lives through John.
You've been very inspirational and just plain special to me. I
learned a great deal in a short time from you—at a time
when I was very vulnerable and open—and your opinions
and ideas really hit home. . . . You are very special, Bobbie,
and soon I know you'll find someone just as wonderful and
wise to share your world with. And even though I'm no
wide-world authority on the topic, I bet whoever it is will
bring a sparkle to your eyes that has perhaps been missing
for a while, and you'll do the same for him. . . . I know how
very happy you and John were, and I just wish for you all of
that happiness and more.

It is hard to think about being open and vulnerable
when wounds are not fully healed. Yet I can't think of a
time in my life—even in the loneliness—when I have
felt more complete than I do right now. Perhaps even
being able to say that is a mark of healing, a moment of
grace.

SEVEN

Grief—With or Without Support

LIVING THROUGH a difficult time, I have found, usually takes so much energy that there is none left for reflection, for the process of discerning meaning. Trying to make sense out of those events is always left for "later."

Even though at the time I could not have given a logical analysis of what I was experiencing in John's dying, death, and my early widowhood, I was aware of two things all the time: grief and support. I experienced anticipatory grief, numbing/shocking grief, and unexpected grief. I was fortunate to have wise people around me.

Many special people during this time have allowed me to talk, to go over and over what happened, to look at the anger and loneliness and resentment and sadness that are mine as a widow. They have listened, encouraged, said the appropriate "uh-huhs." They haven't told me I was silly or that I certainly ought to be "over it" by now. They have just been there for me.

Listening, caring people have themselves been moments of grace. It is hard for me to acknowledge that I am not always strong and able to "handle" widowhood. They have loved me in my weakness and have been very present helps as gifts from God. Each one of them has taught me a little more about trust.

Eight months after John died, Jo appeared at my office. She came with a candle in one hand (to burn to remember her) and a plant in the other (to nurture carefully and help to grow). She and her husband were leaving, moving to Kansas City, and she wanted to say good-bye. She told me I would never know what an impact John and I had had on her, that she had never felt with others the way she felt with us. She told me of the love she sensed in John's room.

Jo is a nurse. She was one of the many that cared for John that last year when it seemed he spent more time in than out of the hospital. Jo was always there with her fantastic, heavy braid of hair keeping time like a metronome on her back as she walked from patient to patient. "Hi, dear," she would say with her twenty-eight years of wisdom as she came on duty. John would grin at her and relax a bit, knowing Jo was in charge for a few hours.

It was Jo who walked around the floor with me not just once, and sat with me at the end of the hall carefully explaining what happens when blood clots form. It was Jo who offered to come in whenever I'd like to

call her, even when it wasn't her shift. It was Jo who
came the morning John died after having worked all
night the night before, just to be there a few minutes
with me.

Even more remarkable, it wasn't *only* Jo. Marty, the
head nurse, encouraged both John and me, kept me
aware of changes, let me talk, sat with John, and held
his hand at times. Marty was able to keep her promise
to John to let him know when the end was near. Very
gently she told him just a few minutes before he died
that it would be soon, that he didn't have much longer
to suffer. Mary Ann and Karen, both experienced
nurses, were confident enough to act swiftly, make
decisions, and hold me up as well.

One after another the nurses and other staff on Two
South were special. They invited me into their lounge
and shared their breaks. They gave me free rein in the
kitchen. They encouraged me as I learned from the
doctors to help administer some of John's special
medication. One of them spoke of the emotional
involvement the nurses deal with. "I'm usually able to
protect myself and keep my distance as people approach death," she told me one day, two weeks before
John's death. "But with John it isn't going to be as easy
for me or the other nurses since we all like him so
much."

Marty invited me to training sessions for the nurses
where they saw tapes of a woman dying at home of
lung cancer, her family close by; a lecture by Leo

Buscaglia on being unafraid to reach others; and a tape
made by a local young man speaking of the death of his
wife, a runner at Iowa State University. John watched
the Buscaglia tape with the group as well. It was ten
days before his death. He knew he had only a few days
left.

Since John was especially concerned about the girls,
as the end drew closer he began to worry about breaking down in front of them. It was then that he called
for Judy Beitz, one of the social workers at the medical
center. She and I had shared some clients in the past,
and now John and I were numbered among those to
whom she so carefully ministered. She was with us a
lot those last two months. He called her to come that
one special time when he was struggling with what to
do about the girls. He was trying to figure out how he
could tell them good-bye and that he loved them, but
he was afraid. He and Judy talked about some specific
things he could try. They explored having him write
what he wanted to say (or dictate it, because by that
time he did not have the strength to write). It was a
strange day, and he was dealing with difficult things.
Judy made it easier for him.

What I am describing here is support, openness,
encouragement, "truth-in-dying"—making sure the
dignity of the person is kept intact. That is what these
people of the hospital were doing. They were creating
an atmosphere in which John and I could share our
anticipatory grief. They knew that was what we were

doing and both of us knew it too. They allowed us to acknowledge it openly and not miss it. I am grateful for their wisdom.

That kind of encouragement of openness and communication is the hallmark of the way Dr. Donald Zaentz approaches his cancer patients. He and his nursing staff have learned over time that those who are able to meet dying openly are the ones who are also able to live. Conversely, those who are unable to meet death lose a quality in their living. Dr. Zaentz and the nurses look for signs of communication between the patient and the "significant other" and nurture them. Where they find no willingness to communicate, they seek to create an atmosphere in which trembling first steps can be taken. One of the nurses wrote me several weeks after John died:

> You two touched my life so much. I remember the first day I saw you—it was at an "I Can Cope" session. I could easily see the love, caring, and total support you two had. It was beautiful and I'll never forget. You truly had something very special.

I know how important in the grief process this supportive environment was. I count myself fortunate that John and I had time to grieve his death together, to hold each other close and know the days in which we could do that were numbered. I count myself fortunate that two weeks before he died—after we had talked about the fact that it was only a matter of days, and after his last blood transfusion when he was feeling its life-giving strength—we took a two-hour pass from the hospital and went for a ride.

It was the perfect Indian summer day in Iowa. Nowhere else I have ever lived has been able to match an Iowa October day. We drove around town looking at those leaf colors that hide the rest of the year. We went out into the country (not toward home—we agreed together that that was too much to bear, to go where we knew we would never be together again) and eventually stopped in the little park where we often had eaten lunch on warm days when we'd ached to get out of our respective offices. It was "our" spot. We sat in the car a long while, my head on John's shoulder. We were sad together, quiet together, peaceful together.

Before I had taken him out of the hospital for the ride I had talked with Dr. Hardy, his surgeon. I was worried about the blood clot in his leg, worried that something might happen while we were away from the hospital. Dr. Hardy put his hands on my shoulders and gently told me, "Bobbie, you've hung in there this far through a lot of things. You realize, don't you, that it would be a blessing for John if he could go quickly from the blood clot. Do you think you could do this one more thing for him and be strong even if he should die out there alone with you?" We went on our outing with my knowing that not only were his days numbered, but possibly even his seconds.

We talked that day about pallbearers and what John

wanted done with some special things. He told me he didn't want flowers at his funeral, but he did want an active memorial fund, not a plaque to get dusty at church. Most of all, he told me, he didn't want to leave me.

Since that time I have spoken to others whose spouses died suddenly without any opportunity to do those things and to those whose spouses, like John, died slowly over many months but took no opportunity to face openly this death. I have heard them express their anger and bewilderment. They spoke of being surprised at how they felt when what they had ignored, happened. I heard "Why me? Why this? How can you do this to me, God?" None of these situations is easy, but my choice would be the way John and I had it. I think our willingness not to deny, not to run away from death, defused the anger I have seen in others who did not or could not be this open.

What I have seen in others has been an attempt to protect the other person. It is almost as if the one dying senses the loss approaching for the one who will remain and doesn't talk about death so as to ease the time for the other. Or the one who will remain doesn't want to make the dying more difficult for the one whose time is short and, therefore, speaks of other things. I have also seen in action that denial— "I am not dying" or "He is not dying"—takes the whole situation out of reality and makes a mockery both of life and death. I have found myself almost

angry at persons I see doing that. I want to shake
them and say, "Don't miss this special time! Don't!
You are setting yourself up for extra grief and anger
and guilt later!"

Tonight I weep for my friend Eileen. This morning
she became a widow for the second time in her sixty-
eight years. Again she will be called to define "alone"
for herself, to test those definitions of who she is that
were the result of her previous struggle. Right now she
is experiencing the numbness that is raw grief's tender
friend. But the day will come too soon when she will
have to face what she feared—"I am alone again."

Eileen has been the mother to me that I haven't had
for the past twenty years. She has been known to say,
"Bobbie, just try hugging people every now and then.
It will be good for you," as she comes close and lets me
know it is OK for me to be me. Eileen sat with me the
day of John's first surgery, just to be there while I
waited. She sat with me again the second time and
prayed with me in the chapel at the hospital. It was
Eileen who told me to open a new checking account in
my own name shortly before John died so that I would
have money available to take care of bills, money that
wouldn't be tied up in an estate. It was Eileen who
called to check on me and remind me to eat regularly.

And now it is Eileen who has lost her beloved Erv
and must be wondering, *How can I do it again?* It is my
turn to comfort her, to stand beside her, to share with
her what I have learned. Each of us is at the same time

the remaining half of a team and a whole person. I already know Eileen will "make it," because I know Eileen. I have known all along that I would "make it" too. But somehow that only heightens the surprise at the hard times, the down times.

Erv's death was not a surprise. He and Eileen both knew it was coming. Yesterday he told her there wouldn't be a tomorrow for him. The last time I saw him he told me good-bye. He didn't use those words. He imparted some wisdom to me regarding job searches and defining a new life for myself. It was good, fatherly advice. We both knew it was his valedictory to me.

When I left Eileen this morning, she said, "I love you, sweetie." I love her too. We share a bond of grief.

I have some understanding of existential aloneness. I realize I could not do the dying for John any more than those around me could do the grieving for me. I now understand even more clearly, however, that it helps to share such ultimate experiences with another. Isolation makes the pain even worse.

Dr. Zaentz, in treating John, told us both at the beginning that he would not lie to us, that he would include us in the decisions that needed to be made and that he would tell us what was happening. He encouraged questions and never avoided the answers. He knew when to be frank and direct, when to laugh, when to divert one or the other of us when the pressure was too much. He let us know his main responsibility was John but always let me feel I was important in the whole process.

The day he told me he could do no more for John, that time was very short, he offered to come in that evening and talk with the girls and me. We met in the chapel at the hospital—Dr. Zaentz, Sue, Sharon, Brenda, Pam, and me. I had told the girls earlier that their dad was close to death. Dr. Zaentz then told them about cancer, how it grows, what it does. He told them what he does to people who have it, and specifically what he had been doing for their dad. He told them he could do no more for John, as much as he would like to. Pam, the youngest at nine, started to cry. He leaned over and comforted her. He told the girls he had come to love John during this year. He told them it was important for them to keep on visiting him, even if he got confused while they were there. It was a moment of grace. We were quiet for a while and then we left the chapel to go to John's room.

Within the hospital setting I have seen and heard anger directed at both nurses and doctors. Nurses were accused of being too slow, ignoring requests for help; doctors, of being cold, uncaring, never there when wanted. Much of this was frustration on the part of the patient or those around. They were angry at their own helplessness or the perceived hopelessness, and it was easy to lash out at those whose "job" it is to care.

Being involved in John's illness, I learned some things about healing and healers. I watched their own feelings enter into their work worlds. I sensed the frustration in Dr. Zaentz the day he told me almost with pain in his voice of the forty-five-minute coffee break/helplessness session he and Dr. Hardy had held the day before trying to figure out something they could do for John. I watched the way my own doctor, George Hegstrom, took extra time and caring with me and stopped in on occasion to check on John while he made his rounds at the hospital. For long hours every day these healers spent themselves on their patients.

Long ago Hippocrates commented about healing. He understood that it takes a long time to happen. Also long ago God spoke through Isaiah about comforting his people. Healing, time, comfort—all important. I took my calligraphy pen and went to work on white parchment:

> Healing is a matter of time. HIPPOCRATES
>
> Comfort, comfort ye my people, says our God. ISAIAH

I made one parchment for Dr. Zaentz and one for Dr. Hegstrom. Their offices are in the same section of the clinic. It was December 19. On my way to get my allergy shots I saw Dr. Zaentz first. He greeted me as usual. "Happy Hannukah!" I said and handed him the rolled-up parchment. He stopped, opened it, and read. "Casey," he said to his nurse, "look at this." Dr. Zaentz turned to me, his eyes serious. "You couldn't have picked a better time. I've got a woman who is dying and there is nothing I can do." A moment of grace.

Next, Dr. Hegstrom. His hands were full of charts when I said, "Merry Christmas," and put the parchment in the pocket of his white coat. He stopped, put down the charts, took my hands, and leaned over and kissed my cheek. "You have a Merry Christmas," he said. "You're due one." I thought to myself as I walked out of the clinic with unexpected tears in my eyes, *Doesn't anyone ever say thanks to those guys?* I hadn't expected that kind of response to a simple gesture.

Today, from my vantage point of "later," I am beginning to see the cost of support to those around me. My coworkers at the office not only had to do extra work that I was unable to do, but they, too, missed John. John's family, who had many more years with and memories of him than I, had their own severe grief. Yet they held me up time and again, blending my tears into their own.

John's sister Priscilla entered into his suffering with trembling. It was not an easy thing for her to do. I don't know how many times she fixed custard and brought it to John. It was one of the very few things he could eat when he was able to eat. During his final hospitalization she was there faithfully at least once a week, and more often two or three times. Sometimes still in her work uniform, she would bring her handwork and sit with me and John. We would talk, laugh, be sad. Often she would insist that I go with her out of the hospital for a meal, and each Wednesday she and John would have a special time together while the girls and I continued our weekly ritual of dinner out. She rubbed his feet, held his hand, took care of his needs, all with such love and caring that one of the pastors in charge of his funeral commented to me that her ministry to John was certainly constant and tender.

I also know how much it affected John. Many times after she left him John would cry, mourning their separation, and comment on what a special sister she was. She kept the final vigil along with me and Keith, sitting on one side of John's bed holding one hand while I held the other.

Because we shared that time of suffering, we cemented a bond between us. While she remains my sister-in-law, she has become my sister-in-love, one more legacy that John left behind. Priscilla and I have continued to share the healing that has begun for us. She wrote to me a few days after John's death:

> The love he has given us we must now share with others more than ever. This is what I would consider a living memorial.

A year later at Christmas she wrote again:

> Bobbie, I know Christmas cannot be an easy time for you, and how I wish there was something we could do to ease the emptiness. *We* feel it too. I have no words of wisdom, but knowing that we *really care* and are *concerned* for *you*, you should feel better immediately!

Priscilla has given me a gift in grief by letting me know over and over that I am part of this family. She has also helped me understand the depth of the grief of other family members.

For me, the hardest person to be with during this grieving process was John's mother. She hurt terribly during his illness and later after his death. She and John were never able to come to a full reconciliation of the things that kept them apart. She had much time to think and brood about his death. She was nearly eighty-three years old when he, her youngest child, died. She was angry that he had been taken from her. She didn't have good answers for *why* and hadn't yet come to her own understanding of *who*. There were many times I felt her anger directly and her pain expressed in angry words. I watched her denial of this reality crumble as she could no longer believe John was not dying. I watched her try to hold on to things as they had been. I tried to understand the dynamics of her grief. I was not often able to do so gracefully. We were not able to comfort each other. It fell to her other children, Priscilla, Rosemary, and Dean and Helen, to take onto themselves the added burden of their mother's grief.

I have seen this family change because of John's death. I suppose all families change when one member dies. I have seen how important it is to grieve together. These people took the place of my own family nearly a thousand miles away and comforted me in my day-to-day pain. My brother, R. C. Sproul, and my cousin, Jeannette Euler, regularly took time to do long-distance co-grieving and encouraging, but it was the Carlsons who were with me. Through these people God made sure I would understand that he cared about comforting.

As the time since John's death lengthens, so does the time between the terribly painful moments. I am still shocked when something triggers a memory or a realization that brings tears to my eyes. I am surprised when someone indicates to me that I have "had so many sad things happen to me." I do not see myself as a tragic figure. On occasion I have sensed surprise in the eyes or voice of another that I am "not over John yet." A flash of pity is imparted toward me. Some of those times I have not handled gracefully. Only those who know me well know to equate my increasing silence or clenched teeth with rising anger. When I sense a dose of "poor Bobbie" coming my way I have learned not to respond. I do nothing, even though more than once I have wanted to say, "You don't know what you are saying. The grieving process is not something to be switched off in just a few months. Healing takes time." But I don't say it unless I sense it might be understood, that this time might be one in which a new perspective might be imparted. Instead, I note the comments and my response inside, storing them away for future reflecting. I chalk up another moment of grace that leads to understanding.

EIGHT
And Then There Was One

I WONDERED if it would ever come—that time of not being so preoccupied with being a widow. It has. I went to the video store and rented a VCR and two movies. It was a Monday, after work. No one else would be with me—no kids, no one. I went home, fixed something to eat, fed the dog, hooked up the VCR, and indulged in four and a half hours of movies. I didn't have to ask anyone's permission. I didn't even have to bargain with someone to determine which movies to get. I had only myself to please. I had never done anything like that before—for me, just me. The kids love it when they are here for a weekend if we get some movies. And it was great on New Year's Eve to watch three with Keith and Judy. But just for me—well, that was something different.

I enjoyed it. I enjoyed the freedom of being able to do it. But watching two movies by myself is not really all that important. The event was a symbol of an even more important reality: There has been a change in my perspective. I am sensing that I am seeing some things and some events differently.

Two images have come to mind recently, two metaphors I have used to express this time. One is the metaphor of being in the desert—alone, isolated, in the void of nothingness, without life, without color. In that desert I was parched. The wind's toy, I was picked up, let fall, picked up, let fall, picked up. . . . I was alone against the elements and I was puzzled, trying to make sense out of what was happening. I had never been more depressed in my life. I was tired; I was frightened; I was lost.

The second metaphor is that of a corner. A number of years ago I felt myself in another "corner" time. What I wrote then speaks to me again:

> *A corner is a place*
> *Where two walls meet.*
> *Most of them have*
> *Insides and outsides.*
> *Things get trapped in corners.*
> *And sometimes people do too. . . .*
>
> *I know*
> *Because I have been in one.*
> *Trapped is not a good thing*
> *To be.*
> *It makes me too little.*
> *I lose the ability to see over*
> *Things.*
>
> *But I've finally begun to*
> *Realize*

That I have been busy
Setting that trap for myself.

I have been shocked—now—
Into the knowledge
That the outside of a
Corner
Is far more freeing
Than the inside.
The outside
Can be turned.
Perhaps I have been
Enabled to risk that.

For two months I struggled. *Who is this nascent woman inside my skin? Do I know her?* Never had I known such fear. I tried to touch God in my prayer time. I couldn't. My words came back to me even more quickly than I sent them out. It was as if a barrier surrounded me. I couldn't get out and no one else could get in. *Well,* I told myself, *if God won't pay any attention to you, don't worry about keeping up your prayer time or your Bible reading. It won't hurt to skip a day or so.* I lost myself in movies, watching my old friends *Star Trek: I, II,* and *III* again. The first time I saw Spock die I was with John and the kids in North Carolina getting ready to introduce our blended family to my uncle and aunt. It was just a movie. This time there was no more John, no more blended family. The pain of that final separation of Captain James T. Kirk and his Vulcan first officer wrenched me apart. People who don't even exist were acting out my being torn from John right before my eyes. It was like watching myself split in half and not being able to stop it. I wept—sobbing aloud, bitterly, in anguish, ravaged by a sense of loss. What *do* I do now?

I wrestled with that for days. I watched the scene over and over, reexamined the relationship between those two fictional men in the series, in films, in books. I felt silly. Here was I, a grown woman, searching *Star Trek* to define my experience.

Right before Spock died he had an interchange with the third member of the triumvirate, Dr. McCoy. Spock touched the doctor and said, "Remember." *Remember.* I knew that word was significant for me. *Remember.* But remember what? Remember who? And then I knew.

My friend Donna Barker was in Texas visiting her daughters. She and I had been working on the Sunday morning bulletins for church. Her husband, Doug, was preaching and I was working on the order of worship, choosing hymns and portions of Scripture that would fit with his text from John 14. Doug was focusing on Christ's peace. I headed the bulletin with John 14:25-27. I read it several times, in several versions. There it was, what I had been looking for, struggling with. Jesus is talking with his disciples:

> "I have told you this while I am still with you. The Helper, the Holy Spirit, whom the Father will send in my name, will teach you everything and **make you remember** all that I have told you.
>
> "Peace is what I leave with you; it is my own peace that I give

you. I do not give it as the world does. Do not be worried and upset; do not be afraid." JOHN 14:25-27 (emphasis added)

The words broke through to me. I heard them all the way inside myself.

It had been only three months since I experienced the sureness of God's providing for me at Christmas— only three months since I'd learned that he *will* provide for me—and I discovered that I had forgotten.

I don't want to be lonely anymore. I don't want to be a widow, thank you. I don't want any more insecurity and worry and loss. I've done my stint. Is it OK if we get on with my life now?

It is difficult to look at those words of Scripture objectively. Encouragement is one of those things John did for me. When I would come to him bruised or puzzled, he would give me a different perspective in love, and I would sigh deeply, knowing it was going to be "all right." Now I know life does not start "Once upon a time . . ." nor does it end "And they lived happily ever after." There is no fairy godmother to wave her wand for me—nor is the cavalry just over the hill. And it isn't a dream.

The pain is real. It is not cured by shopping binges. (I've tried many.) It is not dissipated by work or fantasy. I've seen others try alcohol. That doesn't work either. The question to be turned inside out this time is, "Are you listening to me, God?" I need to ask instead, "Am I listening to you, God?" How can I remember if I don't listen? How else can I gauge God's faithfulness?

In this book I have been talking about the weak spots in my life—security, patience, and control. These are the areas in which it is hardest for me to "Remember!" I decided to do something, to take some action.

God—through his Word—continued to break through to me. Others around me were breaking through as well. I saw my friend walk up the stairs and turn toward me. It was a time for smiles, a fifteen-minute interlude between meetings. He held out his hands to me as I rose, frightened. "Hi," he said. "It's OK. I haven't seen you for a while and just wanted to greet you." Fifteen minutes of talking, just fifteen minutes, and he was gone—he back to his world and I to mine. It was, however, an important moment, a corner turned for me. Others reached out to me, even made contact, but I kept a certain barrier in place. He invaded my space, touched *me* (not physically, but deeply) like no one else has done since John. He was able to awaken the woman. I am glad to know she is still there. He has given me a gift for which I am grateful.

Another crack in my barrier came from Dick Deems. Dick heads Deems Associates and does life/career planning. I have been working with him to define my skills, my goals, my values so that I will be prepared for a change in employment. The process has been both exhilarating and painful. As I struggled to answer questions about where I wanted my life to be heading, I found myself in tears, immobilized. I searched within myself; I asked others to help me look at some areas; I took them to God; I sneaked up on the questions again only to fail again and once more dissolve into tears. I was terrified. Why couldn't I answer those simple questions?

I sat back in my chair, relaxed, cleared my mind, and allowed the images and thoughts to flow freely. Words like *insecure, lonely, afraid* began to surface and then one important sentence:

I've always been the one to get into resonance with the other.

That was Monday night. My meeting with Dick was set for late Friday afternoon. I had work to do. By Thursday night I knew I needed someone to listen to me, to help me sort through some ideas. So I did what John did so many times, headed the half-mile south to Keith and Judy's. I talked, they listened, and then they gave me a new perspective on where I was. What they told me sounded reasonable. It sounded freeing. It sounded like something I could do. I began to realize that what I had done, without realizing it, was to get myself into a holding pattern. I had been waiting. I don't know exactly what it was that I had been waiting for, but I suddenly knew that I couldn't wait for it to happen anymore. I had to make it happen.

Nothing has changed. My normal, everyday uncertainties still remain. There is no knight on a white horse coming to rescue me. But . . . I *have* turned a corner. It is the corner of understanding that I must create my own resonance. I have been giving myself permission to be me, to define me in a new way. It is all right, now, to be me—single. It is also all right to be me—married. I no longer have to be trapped by my farm-locked acre. And, since I no longer *have* to stay here, I can, if I decide that is what I want.

Each of the people I've mentioned has been reflecting a part of me to myself, has been reflecting my growth. They have been patient, and at times they have provided the nudge needed to get me to move. Through them I have seen the Holy Spirit at work, causing me to remember, reminding me to give myself permission to pay attention to what I know I am. He is the one responsible for urging Donna to call me at work that day I returned to CCJ after my six-month absence. She read me a few words from Jeremiah:

> *"I alone know the plans I have for you, plans to bring you prosperity and not disaster, plans to bring about the future you hope for."* JEREMIAH 29:11

I have visited those words many times over this past year. Each time I am renewed by that promise. Not long ago I read a book on Jeremiah, a series of essays on some of the more salient points. It was then that I took a closer look at the whole of chapter 29 and noticed "my verse" in its proper home. But it didn't "click." I had not been able (or *ready?*) to make the switch from the exiled people of Israel to the widow Carlson. Now, after more healing, I can make that verse apply to me.

Jeremiah sent a letter to the priests, prophets, elders, and all the others who had been exiled to Babylonia. Evidently they, too, had been in a holding pattern. God's message to the people through Jeremiah was not the one they expected to hear. I suspect they were looking for the message of rescue, that all would be well and they could soon go "back home." Instead they were told to:

> *Build houses and settle down. Plant gardens and eat what you grow in them. Marry and have children. . . . Work for the good of the cities where I have made you go as prisoners. Pray to me on their behalf, because if they are prosperous, you will be prosperous too.* JEREMIAH 29:5-7

God had a plan that included their learning how to be his people in a different setting. He wanted them to learn that neither the place nor the circumstances defines who he is to them or they to him. He wanted them to learn to trust him and understand he had a plan for them that was actually superior to the one they had figured out for themselves. Need I draw the analogy any further?

It is so clear to me now that I can't imagine how I

missed it for a whole year, other than to say once again that healing is a matter of time. That message was there a year ago, but I had not the eyes to see nor the heart to understand. Once again I am reminded of the faithfulness of God. His Spirit did cause me to "Remember!" when remembering could bring understanding.

Looking back at these moments of grace and at this process of grief and the struggle to make sense out of it, I find again hope and promise. I don't know what comes next. I do know that I am beginning to see myself as "single" rather than as "widow." I am obviously both. I do know that John has left a growing legacy that continues to surface—in me and my new faith and new life, in Lynette who says she will never forget what he was, in Jerry who on committing himself to his risen Lord named John's struggle as a signpost, in person after person whose lives he touched simply, yet with power.

I have also learned that healing from the pain of grief and loss is not an automatic event. It is possible to keep the healing from happening. It takes only ignoring the pain, denying the events, refusing to "go through it." I have watched others who have been widowed change the subject when I ask how they are, move up to the problem and then veer off in some other direction rather than meet the issue.

For those of us, however, who are willing to make a friend of pain, grief, and loss, there is growth, new understanding, and a rich legacy from our special person. So I end where I began:

> *My husband is dead.*
> *I am not.*
> *I must go on,*
> *Not holding on to him,*
> *Gaining identity from him*
> *Even in death,*
> *But understanding*
> *Who I am—*
> *The gift he gave me*
> *At the cost of his life.*
>
> *He didn't die to*
> *Let me live.*
> *But I see in his*
> *Dying*
> *An opening*
> *To life.*
>
> *God gave me John*
> *So I would learn*
> *I am lovable*
> *Even in my unworthiness.*
> *God took John to himself*
> *So I wouldn't make an*
> *Idol*
> *Of him.*
>
> *God knows who I am*
> *And he gives me ways*
> *To learn it as well.*

And perhaps I have been given the grace to remember that the Spirit of God is at work in me causing me to "Remember" and to trust that he indeed has a plan for me. After all, I am his.